THE
WORDS
ESUS   OF

AZARETH

THE WORD

JESUS OF

NAZARETH

BY LEE CANTELON

ISBN-10: 0-9787620-4-5
ISBN-13: 978-0-9787620-4-9

Portions of this work appeared in The Words of Jesus copyright © 1990 R. L. Cantelon

Printed in the United States of America

10 9 8 7 6 5 4 3 2 1

First Edition

TO MY FATHER, WILLARD CANTELON,
A TRUE SERVANT,
AND TO SCOTT CROLLA FOR
BEGINNING THIS CONVERSATION.

Visit *The Words* online at www.thewords.com and www.thewordstoday.com.

This book was the inspiration for *The Sermon on Exposition Boulevard*, an album of songs by Rickie Lee Jones. You can read more about this on her site, www.rickieleejones.com.

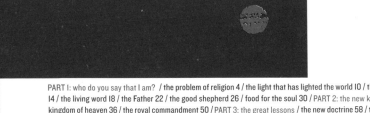

PART I: who do you say that I am? / the problem of religion 4 / the light that has lighted the world 10 / the revelation 14 / the living word 18 / the Father 22 / the good shepherd 26 / food for the soul 30 / PART 2: the new kingdom / the kingdom of heaven 36 / the royal commandment 50 / PART 3: the great lessons / the new doctrine 58 / the blessings 64 / the power of prayer 66 / the treasures in heaven 70 / faith that moves mountains 76 / patience, mercy, and forgiveness 80 / on a fruitful life 86 / health and healing for body and soul 90 / PART 4: the call to a new life / the call 96 / on being born a second time 102 / disciples and servants 108 / the great commission 114 / Christ's prayer for his disciples 120 / PART 5: the promise / this generation 126 / a place for you 130 / the promise of the spirit 132 / an invitation to life 136 / the end times 140 / the return 146 / PART 6: the last days of Christ on the earth / the betrayal 154 / the trial and the cross 158 / following the resurrection 162 / always 166 / index to references 168 / about the author 170 / about the designer 170 / about the book 171 / afterword 172

THE WORDS

JESUS   OF

NAZARETH

WHO DO YOU SAY
THAT I AM?

THE PROBLEM OF RELIGION

TAKE HEED;
BEWARE OF
LIVING YOUR LIFE ON RELIGIOUS "FOOD."

BY NOW YOU HAVE CERTAINLY FORGOTTEN THE FIVE LOAVES THAT FED THE FIVE THOUSAND WITH TWELVE BASKETS LEFT OVER, AND THE SEVEN LOAVES THAT FED THE FOUR THOUSAND AND THE PLENTY THAT REMAINED. BUT I AM NOT SPEAKING TO YOU ABOUT EARTHLY FOOD. NO, I HAVE COME TO WARN YOU AGAINST FEEDING ON THE IDEAS AND FALSE TEACHINGS OF THOSE WHO MARKET IN RELIGION.

IN VAIN SUCH PEOPLE WORSHIP ME, TEACHING AS DOCTRINES WHAT ARE MERELY THE INVENTIONS OF MEN. PREOCCUPIED WITH THEIR OWN SUPERSTITIONS, THEY HAVE FORGOTTEN THE COMMANDMENTS OF GOD.

BEWARE OF FALSE TEACHERS WHO STAND BEFORE YOU WEARING SHEEP'S CLOTHING. BENEATH THEIR GUISE HIDES A RAVENOUS WOLF. THEY FOLLOW THEIR TRUE MASTER, THE EVIL ONE, AND DO WHAT AS HE COMMANDS THEM. HE WAS A MURDERER FROM THE BEGINNING AND NEVER TOLD THE TRUTH, BECAUSE THERE WAS NEVER TRUTH IN HIM. WHEN HE LIES, HE SPEAKS IN CHARACTER, FOR HE IS A LIAR, AND THE FATHER OF LIES.

TO THOSE WHO SET THEMSELVES UP TO BE YOUR JUDGES, I SAY, JUDGMENT UPON YOU, FALSE TEACHERS. HYPOCRITES! YOU, WHO WILL NEVER ENTER THE KINGDOM OF HEAVEN, BAR THE VERY WAY TO THOSE WHO LONG TO GO IN. YOU TRAVEL ACROSS LAND AND SEA TO GAIN ONE PROSELYTE, AND WHEN THAT PERSON IS WON, YOU MAKE THEM TWO TIMES MORE THE CHILD OF HELL THAN YOU ARE YOURSELVES. DO YOU NOT MERIT GREAT DAMNATION?

YOU STEAL FROM THE POOR AND THE WIDOWS, AND THEN, TO CONCEAL YOUR TRUE INTENTIONS, YOU MAKE LONG PIOUS PRAYERS.

YOU DECREE: "THE TEMPLE IS UNIMPORTANT. WHAT IS IMPORTANT IS THE TREASURY OF THE TEMPLE!"

BUT WHICH IS GREATER: THE GOLD IN THE TREASURY, OR THE TEMPLE THAT SANCTIFIES THE GOLD?

AND YOU SAY: "THE ALTAR IS NOT IMPORTANT; BUT THE GIFT THAT IS UPON IT IS IMPORTANT."

YOU ARE BOTH FOOLISH AND BLIND. WHICH IS GREATER: THE GIFT ON THE ALTAR, OR THE ALTAR THAT SANCTIFIES THE GIFT?

WHOEVER HONORS THE ALTAR HONORS IT AND ALL THINGS UPON IT. AND WHOEVER HONORS THE TEMPLE HONORS HIM WHO DWELLS WITHIN ITS WALLS. AND THEY WHO HONOR HEAVEN, HONOR THE THRONE OF GOD, AND HE WHO SITS UPON IT.

YOU MAKE CEREMONIAL OFFERINGS OF EVEN THE HERBS THAT GROW AT YOUR FRONT DOOR. ALL THE WHILE, YOU HAVE FORGOTTEN THE WEIGHTY MATTERS OF THE LAW: JUDGMENT, MERCY, AND FAITH.

YOUR VISION EXTENDS NOT ONE INCH IN FRONT OF YOUR FACE. PIOUSLY YOU STRAIN A GNAT FROM YOUR WINE, AND PROCEED TO SWALLOW A CAMEL. SELF-RIGHTEOUSLY YOU CLEAN THE OUTSIDE OF YOUR CUP, WHILE INSIDE REMAINS THE GRIME OF EXTORTION. HOW BLIND CAN YOU BE! FIRST TAKE CARE OF WHAT IS CONCEALED WITHIN. ONLY THEN WILL THE OUTSIDE BE CLEAN.

FALSE TEACHERS! IN YOUR HYPOCRISY YOU ARE NO BETTER THAN WHITEWASHED TOMBS, WHICH MIGHT APPEAR BEAUTIFUL ON THE OUTSIDE, BUT INSIDE ARE FULL OF DEATH AND DECAYING BONES. YOU MAY IMPRESS PEOPLE BY YOUR SUPERFICIAL DEMONSTRATIONS OF VIRTUE, BUT INSIDE YOU ARE CONSUMED WITH HYPOCRISY AND HAVE FALLEN SHORT OF THE TRUTH. HOW CAN YOU BELIEVE, YOU, WHO LIVE ONLY FOR YOUR COLLEAGUE'S PRAISE, NEVER SEEKING THE HONOR THAT COMES FROM GOD ALONE?

YOU BUILD MONUMENTS TO THE PROPHETS AND PLACE FLOWERS AT THE TOMBS OF THE RIGHTEOUS AND SAY: "IF WE HAD LIVED IN THE DAYS OF OUR ANCESTORS, WE WOULD NEVER HAVE ALLOWED THEIR INNOCENT BLOOD TO BE SHED."

BE WITNESS TO YOUR OWN INCONSISTENCY! YOU ARE THE DESCENDENTS OF THOSE WHO KILLED THE PROPHETS AND HAVE SURPASSED EVEN THEIR WICKED ACTS. SNAKES! GENERATION OF VIPERS! HOW WILL YOU ESCAPE THE CONDEMNATION OF ETERNAL JUDGMENT?

BEHOLD, IN THE DAYS TO COME, I WILL SEND YOU PROPHETS, AND WISE MEN, AND TEACHERS. EVEN THESE YOU WILL KILL AND CRUCIFY. YES, EVEN THESE YOU WILL PERSECUTE, AND PURSUE TO THE ENDS OF THE EARTH.

SUCH HYPOCRISY! ISAIAH WAS RIGHT WHEN HE PROPHESIED OF YOU: "THEY APPROACH ME WITH THEIR MOUTHS, AND HONOR ME WITH THEIR LIPS; BUT THEIR HEARTS ARE FAR FROM ME."

YOU JUSTIFY YOURSELVES BEFORE YOUR CONGREGATIONS, BUT GOD KNOWS THE EVIL INTENTIONS OF YOUR HEARTS: FOR THAT WHICH IS HIGHLY ESTEEMED BY MAN IS REPULSIVE IN THE SIGHT OF GOD.

TAKE HEED: MANY WILL COME FROM THE EAST AND WEST AND ENTER JOYFULLY THE KINGDOM OF HEAVEN. BUT MANY WHO SHOULD HAVE COME IN WILL BE BANISHED INSTEAD TO THE DARKNESS OUTSIDE. BE FOREWARNED: UNLESS YOUR RIGHTEOUSNESS EXCEEDS THE PSEUDO-RIGHTEOUSNESS OF THE RELIGIOUS, YOU WILL NOT SET FOOT INSIDE THE KINGDOM OF HEAVEN.

THE
LIGHT
THAT HAS

iGHTED
THE WORLD.

I HAVE COME TO BE A LIGHT TO THE WORLD, THAT WHOEVER BELIEVES IN ME SHOULD NOT REMAIN IN DARKNESS. I AM THE LIGHT THAT HAS LIGHTED THE WORLD; THEY THAT FOLLOW ME WILL NEVER AGAIN WALK IN DARKNESS, BUT LIVE THEIR LIVES IN THE LIGHT.

ONCE, YOU JOURNEYED INTO THE WILDERNESS TO LISTEN TO JOHN, THE PROPHET YOU CALLED THE BAPTISER. HE SPOKE TO YOU OF THE TRUTH. HE WAS A BURNING AND SHINING LIGHT: AND YOU WERE WILLING, AT LEAST FOR A WHILE, TO FOLLOW HIM. NOW, ONE HAS COME WITH A GREATER DEMONSTRATION OF POWER THAN JOHN, FOR THE WORK THAT MY FATHER HAS GIVEN ME TO ACCOMPLISH, THE VERY ACTS WHICH I PERFORM NOW IN YOUR PRESENCE, PROVE THAT I AM SENT FROM GOD.

IF I DO NOT THE WORKS OF MY FATHER, THEN YOU ARE FREE TO TURN AWAY. BUT, IF I DO HIS WORKS, EVEN IF YOU DON'T BELIEVE IN ME, BELIEVE IN THE WORKS THAT I DO; THAT YOU MAY KNOW AND BELIEVE THAT THE FATHER IS

IN ME AND I AM IN HIM. I MUST DO THE WORK OF HIM WHO SENT ME WHILE IT IS DAY, BECAUSE THE NIGHT IS FAST APPROACHING WHEN NO ONE WILL BE ABLE TO WORK.

THE LAMP OF THE BODY IS THE EYE: IF YOUR EYE IS SOUND, YOUR WHOLE LIFE WILL BE FILLED WITH LIGHT, BUT IF YOUR EYE BE PREOCCUPIED WITH EVIL, YOUR WHOLE LIFE WILL BE OBSCURED WITH DARKNESS. IF WHAT ILLUMINATES YOUR LIFE IS DARKNESS, HOW GREAT AND TERRIBLE IS THAT DARKNESS!

ARE THERE NOT AT LEAST TWELVE HOURS OF DAYLIGHT? IF YOU WALK BY DAY YOU DO NOT STUMBLE, BECAUSE OF THE NATURAL LIGHT AROUND YOU. IF, HOWEVER, YOU WALK BY NIGHT YOU WILL FALL, BECAUSE THERE IS NO DAYLIGHT TO GUIDE YOU. BELIEVE IN THE LIGHT, SO THAT YOU MAY BECOME "CHILDREN OF THE LIGHT." BE ACTIVE WHILE YOU HAVE THE LIGHT PRESENT WITH YOU, FOR DARKNESS IS RAPIDLY FALLING.

THOSE THAT WALK IN DARKNESS ARE THE LOST,

AND IF THE BLIND ARE LEADING THE BLIND, THEN BOTH ARE DESTINED TO FALL.

YOU DO NOT LIGHT A CANDLE AND THEN CONCEAL IT BENEATH A VASE OR PLACE IT UNDER A BED; INSTEAD, YOU SET IT ON A CANDLESTICK, SO THAT YOU OR YOUR GUESTS ENTER A HOUSE FILLED WITH LIGHT. DO YOU NOT REALIZE THAT YOU ARE CALLED OUT TO BE LIGHTS IN THIS WORLD? YOUR LIFE IS SIMILAR TO A CITY BUILT ON A HILL THAT CANNOT GO UNNOTICED. LET YOUR LIGHT THEREFORE SHINE BRIGHTLY BEFORE ALL PEOPLE, THAT THEY MIGHT SEE YOUR GOOD WORKS AND PRAISE YOUR FATHER, WHO IS IN HEAVEN.

THAT WHICH YOU DO IN SECRET WILL EVENTUALLY BE REVEALED, AND THAT WHICH SEEMS TO BE HIDDEN WILL ONE DAY BE BROADCAST FAR AND WIDE. WHAT I AM TELLING YOU NOW IN PRIVATE PROCLAIM PUBLICLY, AND WHAT YOU HEAR WHISPERED BY THE SPIRIT, SHOUT ALOUD FROM THE HOUSETOPS.

THE
REVELA-
TION
THE TIME

IS COME THAT

THE SON OF MAN BE REVEALED AND GLORIFIED.

I DO NOT COME SEEKING MY OWN GLORY; THERE IS ONE WHO SEEKS TO EXALT ME, AND HE IS THE JUDGE OF ALL WHO REJECT ME.

IT IS WRITTEN IN YOUR EARTHLY LAWS THAT THE CONCURRING TESTIMONY OF TWO WITNESSES IS TRUE. ACCORDINGLY, I BEAR WITNESS OF MYSELF, AS DOES MY FATHER WHO HAS SENT ME. I KNOW THAT THE WITNESS HE HAS GIVEN OF ME IS TRUE. BECAUSE OF THIS, I DO NOT HAVE NEED OF THE ENDORSEMENT OF ANY EARTHLY AUTHORITY.

HE WHO SPEAKS ONLY HIS OWN IDEAS DOES SO TO GAIN HONOR FOR HIMSELF. BUT HE WHO WORKS FOR THE GLORY AND HONOR OF THE ONE WHO HAS SENT HIM IS TRUE, AND THERE IS NOTHING FALSE OR VAINGLORIOUS IN HIM.

I HAVE NOT COME TO YOU ON MY OWN BEHALF, BUT HAVE BEEN SENT BY THE ONE WHO IS TRUTH. NOR HAVE I COME DOWN FROM HEAVEN TO DO MY OWN WILL, BUT RATHER TO DO THE WILL OF THE FATHER WHO HAS SENT ME. I WAS BORN

AND CAME INTO THIS WORLD FOR ONE PURPOSE: TO BE A LIVING WITNESS TO THE TRUTH. THOSE WHO LOVE THE TRUTH WILL FOLLOW ME.

I AND MY FATHER ARE ONE. IN HIS NAME I HAVE COME TO YOU THAT YOU MIGHT HAVE LIFE, AND THAT YOU MIGHT HAVE IT MORE ABUNDANTLY.

ALL AUTHORITY IS GIVEN TO ME, BOTH IN HEAVEN AND ON EARTH. I AM ABLE TO GIVE YOU ETERNAL LIFE, THE KEYS TO THE KINGDOM OF HEAVEN, AND POWER OVER ALL DOMINATION OF THE EVIL ONE. NO LONGER BE TROUBLED OR AFRAID. MY PEACE I GIVE TO YOU, A PEACE FAR SURPASSING THAT WHICH THE NATURAL WORLD IS ABLE TO IMPART.

IN ME YOU WILL KNOW THE TRUTH, AND THE TRUTH WILL SET YOU FREE; AND IF THE SON OF GOD SETS YOU FREE, YOU WILL BE FREE INDEED. I TELL YOU THIS SO THAT YOU MIGHT HAVE FAITH TO BELIEVE, AND BE TRANSFORMED.

THIS IS THE WILL OF GOD, THAT EVERYONE WHO LOOKS TO THE SON AND BELIEVES IN HIM WILL HAVE EVERLASTING LIFE. IF YOU BELIEVE IN ME, I WILL RAISE YOU UP ON THE LAST DAY. DO YOU BELIEVE IN THE SON OF GOD? IT IS HE THAT IS SPEAKING TO YOU.

"EVERYONE WHO LOOKS TO THE SON AND BELIEVES IN HIM WILL HAVE EVERLASTING LIFE."

THE
LIVING
WORD

THE FATHER WHO   SENT ME
HAS

INSTRUCTED ME AS TO WHAT I SHOULD TELL YOU. I KNOW THAT HIS WORDS LEAD TO EVERLASTING LIFE; SO WHATEVER HE TELLS ME TO SAY, I SAY.

THESE WORDS THAT I SPEAK ARE NOT MY OWN, BUT COME FROM THE FATHER WHO HAS SENT ME. THEY THAT HEAR THE WORDS THAT I SPEAK AND BELIEVE IN HE THAT HAS SENT ME, WILL HAVE EVERLASTING LIFE. THEY WILL NOT BE CONDEMNED, BUT WILL PASS FROM DEATH TO LIFE.

LISTEN: THE HOUR IS COMING AND HAS ALREADY COME, WHEN EVEN THE DEAD WILL HEAR THE VOICE OF THE SON OF GOD, AND WHOEVER HEARS HIS VOICE SHALL LIVE.

YOU SEARCH THE ANCIENT PROPHETIC WRITINGS BECAUSE YOU ARE SEEKING THE PATH TO ETERNAL LIFE. THE PROPHETS THEMSELVES TESTIFY CLEARLY OF ME. AND YET, YOU HESITATE TO COME TO ME THAT YOU MIGHT FIND NEW LIFE.

THOUGH NOT APPEARING TO YOU PERSONALLY OR SPEAKING TO YOU AUDIBLY, THE FATHER HAS

BORN WITNESS OF ME. BY REFUSING TO BELIEVE IN ME, THE ONE SENT TO YOU BY MY FATHER, YOU CLOSE YOUR EARS FROM HEARING THE VERY VOICE OF GOD. HOW IS IT THAT SOME OF YOU SAY, REGARDING THE ONE WHOM THE FATHER HAS SET APART AS HIS VERY OWN AND SENT INTO THE WORLD, "HE COMMITS BLASPHEMY BECAUSE HE SAYS, 'HE IS THE SON OF GOD'?"

I TELL YOU NOW: I AM THE WAY, THE TRUTH, AND THE LIFE; NO ON CAN RECOGNIZE THE FATHER, EXCEPT BY MY INTRODUCTION. ONLY THE BREATH OF GOD GIVES LIFE. YOUR EARTHLY BODY GROWS OLD AND WILL EVENTUALLY FAIL, BUT THE WORDS THAT I SPEAK TO YOU ARE FILLED WITH GOD'S BREATH AND ARE LIFE.

I DO NOT PASS JUDGMENT ON THOSE WHO HEAR THESE WORDS AND DO NOT BELIEVE; FOR I HAVE NOT COME TO JUDGE THE WORLD, BUT TO RESCUE IT. BE WARNED; THOSE THAT REJECT MY WORDS WILL BE HELD ACCOUNTABLE: THE TRUTH THAT I HAVE SPOKEN WILL STAND AS THEIR JUDGE ON THE LAST DAY.

SURELY THE HEAVENS ABOVE YOU AND THE
EARTH BENEATH YOUR FEET WILL ONE DAY PASS
AWAY; BUT THE WORDS THAT I SPEAK WILL
NEVER PASS AWAY.
"THE WORDS THAT I SPEAK
TO YOU ARE FILLED WITH
GOD'S BREATH
AND ARE
LIFE."

THE FA-
THER
WHAT DO YOU THINK OF

JESUS CHRIST? WHOSE SON IS HE?

NO ONE KNOWS WHO THE SON OF GOD IS, EXCEPT THE FATHER IN HEAVEN: AND NO ONE CAN KNOW WHO THE FATHER IS, EXCEPT THE SON AND THOSE TO WHOM THE SON WILL REVEAL HIM. UNTIL NOW YOU HAVE NOT KNOWN HIM AS I DO; BUT I HAVE COME, SENT FROM HIM TO YOU.

THE ONE WHO HAS SENT ME IS PRESENT WITH ME NOW. THERE IS NO SEPARATION BETWEEN US, FOR I ALWAYS DO WHAT PLEASES HIM. IN FACT, IN SEEING ME YOU HAVE SEEN THE FATHER. WHY THEN DO YOU KEEP SAYING, "REVEAL GOD TO US"? DO YOU NOT BELIEVE THAT I AM ONE, AND EQUAL WITH MY FATHER?

I AND MY FATHER ARE ONE. EVERYTHING THAT THE FATHER HAS IS MINE. I HAVE COME FROM THE FATHER TO THIS WORLD; I WILL LEAVE THIS WORLD AGAIN, AND RETURN TO MY FATHER.

THE SON CAN DO NOTHING ON HIS OWN, BUT DOES ONLY WHAT HE SEES THE FATHER DO. THE

FATHER LOVES THE SON, AND HAS REVEALED TO HIM HIS UNIVERSAL PLAN; AND YOU WILL WITNESS EVEN GREATER MIRACLES THAN THOSE WHICH YOU HAVE ALREADY SEEN. EVEN AS THE FATHER RAISES THE DEAD AND GIVES NEW LIFE, SO THE SON WILL GIVE NEW LIFE TO WHOMEVER HE WILL.

AND YET, I CAN DO NOTHING ON MY OWN; I JUDGE ONLY AS GOD GUIDES ME; MY WAYS ARE PERFECT BECAUSE I SEEK NOT MY OWN WILL, BUT THE WILL OF THE FATHER WHO HAS SENT ME. AS THE FATHER HAS THE POWER TO GIVE LIFE, SO THE SON HAS THE GIFT OF LIFE, AND HAS BEEN GIVEN THE AUTHORITY TO EXECUTE JUDGMENT, BECAUSE HE IS THE MESSIAH, THE SON OF MAN.

I HAVE SAID THIS FROM THE BEGINNING: THERE IS MUCH IN YOUR LIVES THAT I COULD CONDEMN, BUT I HAVE COME WITH ANOTHER MESSAGE, GIVEN TO ME BY THE ONE WHO IS

THE TRUTH. THIS IS THE MESSAGE THAT I SPEAK TO THE WORLD.

WHEN AT LAST YOU LIFT UP THE SON OF MAN (ON THE CROSS), YOU WILL KNOW WHO I AM, REALIZING THAT I DID NOTHING ACCORDING TO MY OWN PLAN OR AUTHORITY, BUT DELIVERED TO YOU THE WORDS WHICH MY FATHER INSTRUCTED ME TO PROCLAIM. "IN SEEING ME, YOU HAVE SEEN THE

FATHER."

THE GOOD SHEPHERD

FEAR NOT,

LITTLE FLOCK, IT IS YOUR FATHER'S GOOD PLEASURE TO GIVE YOU THE KINGDOM.

I AM THE GOOD SHEPHERD. I KNOW MY FLOCK AND THEY KNOW ME, EVEN AS THE FATHER KNOWS ME AND I KNOW THE FATHER. I AM WILLING TO GIVE MY LIFE FOR THE SAKE OF THE SHEEP. MY SHEEP RECOGNIZE MY VOICE. I KNOW THEM EACH BY NAME, AND THEY FOLLOW ME. I GIVE THEM ETERNAL LIFE. THEY WILL NEVER BE DESTROYED, NOR CAN ANYONE TEAR THEM OUT OF MY HAND. MY FATHER, WHO GAVE THEM TO ME, IS GREATER THAN ANY KINGDOM OR POWER, AND NO FORCE IS ABLE TO PLUCK EVEN THE WEAKEST FROM HIS MIGHTY HAND. STILL, THERE ARE MANY SHEEP THAT ARE LOST OUTSIDE THE FOLD: I MUST GATHER THEM AS WELL. THEY TOO WILL REJOICE AT THE SOUND OF MY VOICE AND WILL BECOME MEMBERS OF ONE GREAT FOLD, WITH ONE SHEPHERD TO CARE FOR THEM NIGHT AND DAY.

HE THAT ENTERS IN BY THE FRONT DOOR OF THE FOLD IS THE SHEPHERD OF THE SHEEP. TO HIM THE DOORKEEPER OPENS THE DOOR, AND THE SHEEP THRILL AT THE SOUND OF HIS VOICE. HE CALLS THEM EACH BY NAME, AND LEADS THEM OUT TO GREEN PASTURES. WHEN HE LEADS THE SHEEP OUT TO GRAZE, HE GOES BEFORE THEM. THEY FOLLOW HIM, COMFORTED BY THE WORDS THAT HE SPEAKS. THEY WILL NOT FOLLOW A STRANGER; INSTEAD, THEY RUN FROM THE SOUND OF AN UNFAMILIAR VOICE.

I AM THE GOOD SHEPHERD WHO GIVES MY LIFE FOR THE SHEEP. THE HIRED HAND IS NO SUBSTITUTE. HE DOES NOT CARE FOR THE SHEEP AS IF THEY WERE HIS OWN; AND WHEN THE WOLF COMES HE RUNS AWAY, LEAVING THE SHEEP UNGUARDED. THE WOLF CATCHES THEM, AND THEY ARE SCATTERED.

I AM THE DOOR TO THE SHEEPFOLD. THOSE WHO ATTEMPT TO ENTER THIS FOLD BY ANY

OTHER WAY ARE THIEVES AND ROBBERS. MANY
IMPOSTERS HAVE COME BEFORE ME, BUT THE
SHEEP DID NOT RECOGNIZE OR FOLLOW THEM.
I AM THE DOOR. ENTER BY THIS DOOR AND YOU
WILL BE SAFE, FREE TO GO IN AND OUT AND FIND
FOOD.

THIS EARTH IS PLAGUED BY CORRUPTION, BY DEATH
AND DESTRUCTION. I HAVE COME TO UNDO THIS
CURSE, THAT YOU MIGHT DISCOVER THE TRUE
MEANING OF LIFE AND BE BLESSED.
"I AM THE GOOD SHEPHERD
WHO GIVES   MY   LIFE   FOR
THE SHEEP."

FOOD FOR THE SOUL

IT IS WRITTEN: "MAN SHALL
NOT

LIVE BY BREAD ALONE, BUT BY EVERY WORD THAT PROCEEDS OUT FROM THE MOUTH OF GOD."

I AM THE BREAD OF LIFE: IF YOU COME TO ME, YOU WILL NEVER AGAIN HUNGER SPIRITUALLY; AND IF YOU BELIEVE IN ME, YOU WILL NEVER AGAIN KNOW SPIRITUAL THIRST. RISE UP! TAKE HOLD OF THE LIVING BREAD, THE SPIRITUAL BREAD THAT HAS COME DOWN FROM HEAVEN: IF YOU EAT OF THIS BREAD, YOU WILL LIVE FOREVER. THE BREAD THAT I OFFER YOU IS MY LIFE, WHICH I GIVE FOR THE LIFE OF THE WORLD. I AM THE BREAD OF LIFE COME DOWN FROM HEAVEN SO THAT YOU MAY FEAST ON SPIRITUAL FOOD, AND BECAUSE OF THIS RECEIVE SPIRITUAL LIFE AND NOT DIE.

ALL OF YOUR ENERGIES ARE SPENT IN THE PURSUIT OF FOOD THAT PERISHES; INSTEAD, SEEK SPIRITUAL FOOD THAT WILL ENDURE FOREVER. THIS IS THE FOOD THAT I LONG TO GIVE YOU, FOR GOD THE FATHER HAS GIVEN ME THIS POWER.

SINCE CHILDHOOD YOU HAVE HEARD THE STORY OF HOW YOUR ANCESTORS ATE MANNA IN THE DESERT, BUT THAT WAS LONG AGO, AND NOW THEY ARE ANCIENT MEMORIES. IN SPITE OF THOSE MIRACLES, MOSES WAS NOT ABLE TO PROVIDE THE TRUE BREAD OF HEAVEN, THAT WHICH MY FATHER IS OFFERING TO YOU NOW. FOR THE BREAD OF GOD IS EMBODIED IN THE ONE WHO IS SPEAKING TO YOU, WHO HAS COME DOWN FROM HEAVEN, AND OFFERED HIS OWN LIFE FOR THE WORLD.

IF YOU UNDERSTOOD THIS, YOU WOULD BEG ME TO GIVE YOU LIVING WATER AS WELL; FOR WHOEVER DRINKS NATURAL WATER SOON THIRSTS AGAIN, BUT WHOEVER DRINKS OF

THE WATER THAT I GIVE WILL DISCOVER A WELL THAT SPRINGS UP WITHIN, OVERFLOWING WITH ETERNAL LIFE.

ARE YOU THIRSTING SPIRITUALLY? COME TO ME AND DRINK; FOR THEY THAT BELIEVE IN ME, AS IT HAS BEEN WRITTEN, "OUT OF THEIR INNERMOST BEING WILL FLOW RIVERS OF LIVING WATER."

THE NEW KING-
DOM

THE KINGDOM OF HEAV-EN

SINCE THE TIME OF JOHN
THE BAPTISER UNTIL

NOW, THE KINGDOM OF HEAVEN HAS BEEN FORCEFULLY ADVANCING, AND GREAT IS THE NUMBER THAT EAGERLY, AND IN DESPERATION, HAVE SEIZED HOLD OF ITS TRUTH.

THE KINGDOM OF HEAVEN CAN BE LIKENED TO A FARMER'S WHEAT FIELD, PLANTED WITH GOOD SEED. ONE NIGHT, WHILE THE FARMER SLEPT, HIS ENEMY CAME AND SOWED DARNEL WEEDS AMONG THE WHEAT. WHEN THE FIRST BLADES OF WHEAT FINALLY PUSHED UP THROUGH THE EARTH, WEEDS APPEARED ALONGSIDE. SEEING THIS, THE SERVANTS RUSHED TO THE FARMER, AND WITH DISTRESSED VOICES WEPT: "SIR, DID NOT WE SOW GOOD SEED IN YOUR FIELD? WHY THEN ARE THERE SO MANY DARNEL WEEDS?"

THE FARMER ANSWERED: "AN ENEMY HAS DONE THIS."

"SHALL WE TRY TO REMOVE THEM?" THE SERVANTS ASKED.

"NO," THE FARMER REPLIED. "IF YOU PULL UP THE WEEDS, YOU WILL UPROOT THE WHEAT AS WELL. LET THEM BOTH GROW TOGETHER UNTIL THE HARVEST TIME; AND AT THE TIME OF THE HARVEST I WILL INSTRUCT THE REAPERS AS FOLLOWS: 'GATHER FIRST THE WEEDS, AND BIND THEM INTO BUNDLES FOR BURNING. THEN GATHER THE WHEAT INTO MY STOREHOUSE.'"

HERE IS THE LESSON: HE THAT SOWED THE GOOD SEED IS THE SON OF MAN. THE FIELD IS THE WORLD. THE GOOD SEED REPRESENTS THE CHILDREN OF THE KINGDOM, WHILE THE REMAINING SEEDS REPRESENT THOSE DECEIVED BY THE WICKED ONE. THE ENEMY THAT PLANTED THE WEEDS IS THE EVIL ONE. THE HARVEST IS THE END OF THE WORLD, AND THE REAPERS ARE THE ANGELS. JUST AS THE DARNEL WEEDS WERE GATHERED AND BURNED IN THE FIRE, SO WILL IT BE AT THE END OF THIS AGE. THE SON OF MAN WILL SEND HIS ANGELS, AND THEY WILL GATHER EVERYTHING THAT HAS CAUSED HUMANKIND TO STUMBLE AND THOSE WHO LIVE LAWLESSLY OUTSIDE OF THE KINGDOM, AND WILL EXILE THEM TO A PLACE OF WEEPING AND REGRET. THEN THE RIGHTEOUS WILL SHINE AS BRIGHTLY AS THE SUN IN THE KINGDOM OF THEIR FATHER. IF YOU HAVE EARS TO HEAR, THEN HEAR THESE WORDS.

EVERY KINGDOM THAT IS DIVIDED AGAINST ITSELF IS DOOMED, AND EVERY CITY OR HOUSE DIVIDED AGAINST ITSELF WILL EVENTUALLY FALL. LIKEWISE, IF THE EVIL ONE IS FIGHTING EVIL, HE IS DIVIDED AGAINST HIMSELF, AND HIS KINGDOM WILL NOT LAST.

ONE CANNOT BE LIBERATED FROM THE KINGDOM OF THE EVIL ONE WITHOUT FIRST BINDING HIS POWER. IF I CAST OUT

DEVILS AND PERFORM SIGNS AND WONDERS AS AN ALLY OF THE DEVIL, AS SOME OF YOU ACCUSE ME, THEN BY WHAT POWER DO YOUR CHILDREN DO THE SAME?

LET YOUR CHILDREN STAND BEFORE YOU AS YOUR JUDGES; THEY CAN SETTLE THIS DISPUTE, FOR IF YOUR CHILDREN CAST OUT DEVILS BY THE BREATH OF GOD, THEN THE KINGDOM IS INDEED COME TO DWELL AMONG YOU.

HAVE YOU EVER HEARD THIS READING FROM THE SCRIPTURES: "THE STONE WHICH THE BUILDERS HAVE REJECTED HAS BECOME THE HONORED CORNERSTONE; THIS IS THE LORD'S DOING, AND MARVELOUS IN OUR EYES"? BEHOLD, THE KINGDOM OF GOD WILL BE TAKEN FROM YOU WHO LISTEN AND DO NOTHING, AND WILL BE GIVEN TO A PEOPLE WORKING TO BRING FORTH FRUIT IN THEIR LIVES.

BEWARE OF HOW YOU TREAT THIS MESSAGE, FOR ALL OF THE SINS OF HUMANKIND WILL BE FORGIVEN, ALONG WITH ALL OF THEIR BLASPHEMIES. BUT THERE IS NO RECONCILIATION FOR THOSE WHO, SEEING EVIL AS GOOD AND GOOD AS EVIL, BLASPHEME THE HOLY SPIRIT. THIS TRANSGRESSION IS ETERNAL. HEED THESE WORDS. ALL ABOUT YOU, EVIL MEN AND PROSTITUTES ARE ENTERING THE KINGDOM OF HEAVEN AHEAD OF YOU. THESE HAVE HEARD THE CALL TO LIFE AND

HAVE TURNED TO GOD, WHILE THE PIOUS AND RELIGIOUS HAVE HEARD THE CALL AND HAVE DELIBERATELY TURNED AWAY.

PRAYER IS NOT ACHIEVED BY REPETITION. IT IS NOT BY REITERATING "LORD, LORD," THAT YOU WILL ENTER THE KINGDOM OF HEAVEN, BUT BY DOING THE WILL OF MY FATHER WHO IS IN HEAVEN.

IF AFTER MIDNIGHT, YOU APPROACHED THE DOOR TO ONE OF THE CITY'S PROMINENT HOUSES LONG AFTER THE OWNER HAD GONE TO BED, AND BEGAN TO KNOCK LOUDLY, AND SHOUT: "OPEN THE DOOR, I WANT TO COME IN," HOW DO YOU THINK YOU WOULD BE RECEIVED?

MOST LIKELY, THE OWNER OF THE HOUSE WOULD SHOUT BACK, "GO AWAY! I DON'T KNOW WHO YOU ARE, OR WHY YOU ARE DISTURBING ME AT THIS HOUR!"

WHAT IF YOU PROTESTED IN REPLY, "BUT WE HAVE EATEN AT THE SAME TABLES, AND OFTEN I HAVE HEARD YOU TEACH IN THE TEMPLE!"

TO THIS THE OWNER MIGHT REPLY, "HEAR MY WORDS; I TELL YOU I DO NOT KNOW YOU. LEAVE ME IN PEACE!"

EVEN SO, ON THE DAY OF JUDGMENT, MANY WILL COME WITH A SIMILAR COMPLAINT, SAYING, "LORD, LORD, HAVEN'T WE PROPHESIED IN YOUR NAME, AND IN YOUR NAME CAST OUT DEVILS, AND IN YOUR NAME ACCOMPLISHED MANY WONDERFUL WORKS?"

THE LORD HIMSELF WILL REPLY, "DEPART. I DO NOT KNOW YOU, WHO HAVE LIVED YOUR ENTIRE LIVES IN DARKNESS."

I INSTRUCT YOU WITH THESE STORIES BECAUSE IT IS GIVEN TO YOU TO UNDERSTAND THE MYSTERIES OF THE KINGDOM OF HEAVEN.

HERE IS ANOTHER PARABLE THAT ILLUSTRATES THE KINGDOM: ONCE THERE LIVED A RICH INVESTOR WHO WAS PREPARING TO DEPART FOR A DISTANT COUNTRY. BEFORE LEAVING, HE CALLED TOGETHER THREE ASSOCIATES, PUTTING THEM IN CHARGE OF MANAGING HIS INVESTMENTS DURING HIS ABSENCE. HE GAVE FIVE ACCOUNTS TO ONE, TWO LESSER ACCOUNTS TO THE OTHER, AND TO THE THIRD HE GAVE ONE INSIGNIFICANT ACCOUNT, RESPONSIBILITIES EQUAL TO THEIR LEVELS OF EXPERIENCE.

SO IT HAPPENED THAT THE ASSOCIATE WHO HAD BEEN ENTRUSTED WITH FIVE ACCOUNTS IMMEDIATELY BEGAN TO BUY AND SELL, AND BEFORE LONG, HE HAD DOUBLED HIS

HOLDINGS, SO THAT HIS ACCOUNTS WERE NOW TEN INSTEAD OF FIVE. THE SECOND ASSOCIATE DID LIKEWISE, INVESTING HIS TWO ACCOUNTS UNTIL HE HAD MADE FOUR FROM THE TWO ENTRUSTED TO HIM. BUT THE THIRD ASSOCIATE DID NOTHING. SO FEARFUL WAS HE THAT HE LOCKED HIS ACCOUNT IN A STRONGBOX AND BURIED IT IN THE GROUND, TERRIFIED THAT IT MIGHT BE TAMPERED WITH, LOST, OR STOLEN.

A GOOD WHILE LATER, THE RICH MAN RETURNED FROM HIS TRIP. IMMEDIATELY HE SUMMONED HIS THREE ASSOCIATES, CURIOUS TO LEARN HOW THEY HAD MANAGED HIS MONEY DURING HIS ABSENCE.

THE FIRST ASSOCIATE RECOUNTED HOW HE HAD INVESTED THE FIVE ACCOUNTS AND NOW HAD TEN. AT THIS THE RICH MAN SAID: "YOU HAVE DONE WELL, AND PROVED FAITHFUL. BECAUSE YOU HAVE BEEN TRUSTWORTHY WITH THE FIVE ACCOUNTS THAT I GAVE YOU, I WILL PUT MORE IMPORTANT ONES UNDER YOUR TRUST. YOU MAY BEGIN TODAY TO BENEFIT FROM THESE RESPONSIBILITIES."

THEN THE RICH MAN CALLED THE SECOND ASSOCIATE, WHO REPORTED: "YOU PUT TWO ACCOUNTS INTO MY CARE; NOW I HAVE FOUR."

HEARING THIS, THE RICH MAN REPEATED WHAT HE HAD SAID TO THE FIRST ASSOCIATE: "WELL DONE! YOU HAVE BEEN FAITHFUL IN MANAGING TWO MINOR ACCOUNTS. I WILL PUT YOU IN CHARGE OF MANY MORE. GO TO YOUR TASK WITH HAPPINESS."

FINALLY, THE THIRD ASSOCIATE WAS CALLED, AND IMMEDIATELY CONFESSED: "I HAVE ALWAYS THOUGHT OF YOU AS A DIFFICULT MAN. YOU COLLECT PROFITS FROM OTHER PEOPLE'S MONEY, AND I FIGURED THAT YOU WOULD ONLY TAKE BACK WHATEVER PROFITS I MIGHT MAKE FROM MY INSIGNIFICANT ACCOUNT. I BURIED MY ACCOUNT IN THE GROUND, WHERE IT HAS REMAINED UNHARMED UNTIL YOUR RETURN."

TO THIS, THE RICH MAN ANSWERED: "FOOLISH ASSOCIATE. YOU KNOW THE MANNER IN WHICH I CONDUCT MY AFFAIRS. AT THE VERY LEAST YOU COULD HAVE ENTRUSTED YOUR ACCOUNT WITH THE CURRENCY DEALERS. ONLY ONE ACCOUNT WAS ASSIGNED TO YOUR CARE, AND YOU HAVE CHOSEN TO BURY IT IN THE GROUND. NOW EVEN THIS WILL BE TAKEN FROM YOU AND GIVEN TO THE OTHERS WHO DID WISELY. WHAT IS LEFT TO YOU, EXCEPT TO DWELL ON YOUR OWN REGRETS?"

IN THE KINGDOM OF HEAVEN, THOSE WHO USE WHAT THEY POSSESS, NO MATTER HOW INSIGNIFICANT IT MIGHT SEEM AT THE TIME, WILL CONTINUE TO RECEIVE MORE AND MORE. ABUNDANCE WILL BE THEIRS! BUT THOSE WHO ACT IN FEAR, UNFAITHFUL IN THE LEAST OF LIFE'S MATTERS, WILL EVENTUALLY LOSE ALL.

ANOTHER EXAMPLE IS FOUND IN THE STORY OF A LANDOWNER. EARLY ONE MORNING, HE WENT OUT TO HIRE WORKERS FOR HIS VINEYARD. FINDING THE SKILLED LABORERS HE NEEDED, HE AGREED WITH THEM ON A WAGE OF ONE SILVER COIN PER DAY. THE CONTRACT ACCEPTED, HE SENT THEM INTO HIS VINEYARD TO WORK.

LATER THAT SAME MORNING, THE LANDOWNER RETURNED TO THE TOWN. SEEING A GROUP OF UNEMPLOYED STANDING IDLE IN THE MARKETPLACE, HE SAID TO THEM: "COME WORK IN MY VINEYARD. I WILL PAY YOU A FAIR DAILY WAGE."

LIKEWISE, AT NOON THE LANDOWNER WENT BACK INTO TOWN, AND THEN AGAIN, MUCH LATER IN THE AFTERNOON. ON EACH OCCASION, HE HIRED THE UNEMPLOYED TO WORK IN HIS VINEYARD. FINALLY, TOWARDS EVENING, HE MET A FEW STRAGGLERS THAT REMAINED WITHOUT WORK, AND ASKED: "WHY DID YOU STAND HERE IDLE?"

THEY RESPONDED: "BECAUSE NO ONE CAME TO HIRE US."

HE SAID: "GO NOW, I STILL HAVE WORK FOR YOU TO DO IN MY VINEYARD."

NIGHT FELL, AND THE LANDOWNER INSTRUCTED THE VINEYARD MANAGER TO CALL THE WORKERS IN FROM THE VINEYARD WHERE THEY WERE WORKING, AND TO GIVE TO EACH OF THEM THEIR WAGES, BEGINNING WITH THE LAST THROUGH TO THE FIRST THAT HAD BEEN HIRED THAT DAY.

THOSE HIRED LAST STEPPED FORWARD, AND EACH RECEIVED A SILVER COIN AS THEIR WAGE. SEEING THIS, THOSE HIRED EARLY THAT MORNING IMAGINED THAT THEY WOULD RECEIVE MORE. WHEN THEIR TURN CAME, HOWEVER, THEY TOO RECEIVED ONE SILVER COIN EACH.

AT THIS THEY BEGAN TO COMPLAIN TO THE LANDOWNER: "UNFAIR! THOSE STRAGGLERS THAT YOU HIRED BARELY WORKED ONE HOUR, AND YOU HAVE PAID THEM ON THE SAME SCALE! WE ARE THE ONES WHO HAVE DONE MOST OF THE WORK, TOILING DURING THE HOTTEST HOURS OF THE DAY!"

BUT THE LANDOWNER ANSWERED: "FRIENDS, I HAVE DONE YOU NO INSULT. DID NOT YOU HAPPILY AGREE ON A DAY'S WAGE OF ONE SILVER COIN? SO TAKE WHAT IS YOURS AND BE ON

YOUR WAY. I HAVE, FROM THE GOODNESS OF MY HEART, PAID THOSE HIRED AT THE END OF THE DAY THE SAME WAGE. HAVE I NOT THE RIGHT TO DO WITH MY MONEY AS I WISH? ARE YOUR EYES SO FULL OF ENVY BECAUSE YOU SEE ME BEING GENEROUS AND KIND?"

THIS TOO, IS A PARABLE OF THE KINGDOM OF HEAVEN; UNDERSTAND IT, FOR THE LAST WILL BE FIRST AND THE FIRST LAST. MANY ARE CALLED, BUT SADLY, FEW ARE CHOSEN.

THE KINGDOM OF HEAVEN IS LIKE A TREASURE BURIED IN A FIELD. ONE DAY, A POOR MAN DISCOVERED IT. IMMEDIATELY HE COVERED IT OVER, AND THEN JOYFULLY SOLD EVERYTHING HE POSSESSED, CONSIDERING THIS A SMALL SACRIFICE, IN ORDER TO PURCHASE THE FIELD WHERE THE TREASURE LAY HIDDEN.

THOSE WHO ENTER THE KINGDOM OF HEAVEN DO NOT ALLOW ANY OF THEIR FORMER, EARTHLY CONCERNS TO DETER THEM. LIKE THE MERCHANT WHO SEARCHED HIS ENTIRE LIFE FOR A PEARL OF GREAT PRICE, THEY JOYFULLY SACRIFICE ALL IN ORDER TO POSSESS SUCH A PRICELESS TREASURE – NEW LIFE, A NEW WAY OF THINKING AND BEING, AND HOPE IN THIS WORLD, AND IN THE WORLD TO COME.

THE KINGDOM OF GOD MOVES FORWARD BY DIVINE COMMAND. THE FARMER SOWS SEED IN HIS FIELD, AND WHEN HIS DAY'S WORK IS DONE HE GOES TO HIS BED. EACH NEW DAY HE RISES AGAIN AND WORKS UNTIL NIGHT FALLS. ALL THE WHILE, THE NATURAL ORDER OF THE EARTH IS AT WORK. THE SEEDS SPROUT AND BEGIN THEIR GROWTH, A SYNTHESIS SO COMPLEX THAT IT IS BEYOND THE FARMER'S ABILITY TO UNDERSTAND IT. TENDER BLADES APPEAR THEN EARS OF CORN UNTIL WHAT WAS PLANTED IS A MATURE CROP, AND THE FARMER TAKES UP HIS SICKLE, FOR THE HARVEST TIME HAS COME.

THE KINGDOM OF HEAVEN IS LIKE A MUSTARD SEED, THE SMALLEST OF NATURE'S KERNELS, FROM WHICH GROWS A GREAT PLANT, AS TALL AS A TREE, A PLACE FOR THE BIRDS TO PERCH AND FIND SHELTER.

THE WORKINGS OF THE KINGDOM CAN BE COMPARED TO A PINCH OF YEAST USED TO MAKE BREAD. EVEN MIXED INTO A GREAT QUANTITY OF FLOUR, IT LEAVENS THROUGHOUT.

LIKE A FISHERMAN'S NET LOWERED INTO THE SEA, THE KINGDOM OF HEAVEN GATHERS UP EVERY VARIETY OF FISH. WHEN IT IS FULL, THE NET IS PULLED BACK ONTO THE SHORE. THERE THE GOOD CATCH IS COLLECTED INTO BASKETS, AND

THE IMPERFECT IS DISCARDED. SO IT WILL BE AT THE END OF THIS AGE. ANGELS WILL SEPARATE THE WICKED FROM AMONG THE CHILDREN OF GOD, EXILING THEM TO A PLACE OF GREAT SORROW.

WITHOUT MATERIAL GOODS, MONEY, OR SUPPORT, I HAVE SENT YOU OUT AS WITNESSES. EQUIPPED WITH THE MESSAGE OF NEW LIFE, YOU HAVE BLESSED OTHERS. DID YOU ONCE LACK FOR ANYTHING?

DO NOT ALLOW YOUR WORRIES TO CONSUME TOMORROW, FOR TOMORROW WILL TAKE CARE OF ITSELF. SURELY THERE IS ENOUGH TO CONCERN YOU EACH DAY WITHOUT FRETTING ABOUT THE FUTURE. WHICH OF YOU BY MENTAL EFFORT CAN ADD ONE INCH TO YOUR HEIGHT?

CONSIDER THE BIRDS OF THE AIR. THEY ARE NOT CONSUMED WITH WORRY. AT NIGHT THEY SLEEP SOUNDLY, KNOWING THAT THEIR HEAVENLY FATHER CARES FOR THEM. DO YOU NOT MATTER MORE THAN THE BIRDS?

ARE NOT TWO SPARROWS SOLD IN THE MARKETPLACE FOR A FEW PENNIES? STILL, ONE OF THEM CANNOT FALL TO THE GROUND WITHOUT YOUR HEAVENLY FATHER'S KNOWLEDGE. CEASE BEING AFRAID. YOU ARE OF GREATER VALUE THAN

MANY FLOCKS OF SPARROWS. EVEN THE VERY HAIRS OF YOUR HEAD ARE NUMBERED.

WHY THEN WORRY ABOUT WHAT YOU WILL WEAR? CONSIDER THE LILIES GROWING WILD IN THE FIELDS, BLOOMING WITHOUT EFFORT. EVEN KING SOLOMON IN ALL OF HIS GLORY WAS NOT ARRAYED AS BEAUTIFULLY AS ONE OF THESE. IF GOD HAS SO CARED FOR THAT WHICH GROWS WILD IN THE FIELD, WHICH IS ALIVE TODAY AND TOMORROW IS CAST INTO THE FIRE, WILL HE NOT CARE FOR YOU MUCH MORE? HOW CAN YOU HAVE SUCH LITTLE FAITH?

THEREFORE, STOP SAYING: "WHAT WILL I EAT? WHAT WILL I DRINK? WILL I EVER HAVE ENOUGH TO CLOTHE MYSELF?" THIS IS HOW THE FAITHLESS THINK, ANXIOUS FOR EVERYTHING. BE AT PEACE! YOUR HEAVENLY FATHER KNOWS THAT YOU HAVE NEED OF ALL OF THESE THINGS, AND MORE.

"SEEK FIRST THE KINGDOM OF GOD AND HIS RIGHTEOUSNESS,   AND ALL OF YOUR NEEDS WILL BE   PROVIDED."

THE ROYAL COMMANDMENT

THE MOST IMPORTANT OF

ALL OF THE

COMMANDMENTS IS THIS: YOU SHALL LOVE THE LORD YOUR GOD WITH ALL OF YOUR HEART, AND WITH ALL OF YOUR SOUL, AND WITH YOUR ENTIRE MIND, AND WITH ALL OF YOUR STRENGTH.

LET THE SECOND COMMANDMENT THEN BE: LOVE YOUR NEIGHBOR AS YOU LOVE YOURSELF.

THIS IS MY COMMANDMENT: THAT YOU LOVE ONE ANOTHER AS I HAVE LOVED YOU! THERE IS NO GREATER LAW, AND THERE IS NO GREATER LOVE MANIFEST THAN THE ACT OF GIVING UP ONE'S LIFE FOR A FRIEND.

WHOEVER LIVES CONTRARY TO THIS COMMANDMENT WILL BE LEAST IN THE KINGDOM OF HEAVEN. BUT WHOEVER ABIDES BY THIS LAW, TEACHING OTHERS THE JOY OF OBEDIENCE, WILL BE CALLED GREAT IN THE KINGDOM OF HEAVEN. I HAVE TOLD YOU ALL OF THESE THINGS THAT MY JOY MIGHT REMAIN WITH YOU, AND THAT YOUR JOY MIGHT BE FULL.

YOU HAVE HEARD IT SAID, "IT IS ONLY RIGHT TO LOVE YOUR FRIENDS AND HATE YOUR ENEMIES."

BUT I ASK YOU TO LOVE YOUR ENEMIES. BLESS THOSE WHO CURSE YOU. SHOW GOODNESS TO THOSE WHO HATE YOU. PRAY FOR THOSE WHO DESPISE AND MISTREAT YOU. DOING THIS, YOU WILL BECOME THE CHILDREN OF YOUR FATHER IN HEAVEN; FOR HE MAKES THE SUN TO RISE ON THE EVIL AND THE GOOD, AND SENDS RAIN TO REFRESH THE JUST AND THE UNJUST. IF YOU LOVE ONLY THOSE WHO LOVE YOU IN RETURN, WHERE IS THE REWARD? EVEN THE CORRUPT LIVE BY THESE RULES.

INSTEAD, LOVE ONE ANOTHER AS I HAVE LOVED YOU. DOING THIS, EVERYONE WILL REALIZE THAT YOU ARE MY DISCIPLES, BECAUSE YOUR LIVES ARE FILLED WITH ACTS OF SELFLESS LOVE. DO NOT BE DECEIVED: IF YOU SAY THAT YOU TRULY LOVE ME, YOUR LIFE WILL BE LIVED ACCORDING TO MY WORDS AND YOU WILL BE HONORED BY MY FATHER AND BLESSED WITH

HIS PRESENCE.

IF YOU HEAR MY WORDS AND ACT ACCORDINGLY, YOU WILL BE LOVED BY MY FATHER AND BY ME AS WELL, AND WE WILL COME AND MAKE OUR DWELLING WITH YOU.

GOD LOVES YOU BECAUSE YOU HAVE BELIEVED IN ME, HIS SON, AND UNDERSTOOD THAT I AM COME TO YOU FROM HIM. PRACTICE THIS AWARENESS. KEEP MY WORDS, AND LIVE IN THIS LOVE, EVEN AS I FOLLOW MY FATHER'S LAWS, AND BY DOING SO, ABIDE CONTINUALLY IN HIS LOVE.

ONCE A MAN TRAVELED FROM JERUSALEM TO JERICHO. THE ROUTE WAS DANGEROUS AND NOTORIOUSLY PLAGUED BY THIEVES. SUCH EVIL MEN ATTACKED HIM, STRIPPED HIM OF HIS POSSESSIONS AND CLOTHES, AND LEFT HIM HALF-DEAD. THE FIRST TO FIND HIM WAS A TEMPLE PRIEST JOURNEYING ALONG THE SAME ROUTE. SEEING THE MAN LYING THERE, HE CROSSED OVER TO THE OTHER SIDE OF THE PATH, AND HURRIED AWAY.

SOME TIME PASSED. A SECOND MAN APPROACHED, ONE WHO PRIDED HIMSELF IN HIS RELIGIOUS OBSERVANCE. SEEING THE WOUNDED MAN, HE HARDENED HIS HEART. GATHERING HIS COAT ABOUT HIM, HE MADE A WIDE DETOUR TO AVOID THE UNPLEASANT SCENE.

TOWARD EVENING, A THIRD MAN DREW NEAR, A POOR SAMARITAN, OUTCAST BECAUSE OF HIS RACE, AND DESPISED AMONG SOCIETY. HE TOO, SAW THE INJURED MAN AND IMMEDIATELY HIS HEART WAS FILLED WITH COMPASSION. TEARING HIS CLOTHING INTO STRIPS, HE BANDAGED THE MAN'S WOUNDS, DRESSING THEM AS BEST AS HE COULD, USING HIS OWN OIL AND WINE. WITH CARE, HE PLACED THE MAN ONTO HIS MULE, AND WENT IN SEARCH OF AN INN. THERE HE MADE SURE THAT ALL OF THE WOUNDED MAN'S NEEDS WOULD BE MET.

IN THE MORNING, BEFORE LEAVING, HE PAID THE INNKEEPER IN ADVANCE AND SAID: "ATTEND TO THE

INJURED MAN, AND WHEN I PASS THIS WAY AGAIN, I WILL REIMBURSE ANY ADDED EXPENSE."

WHICH OF THE THREE DO YOU THINK WAS A NEIGHBOR TO THE MAN WHO FELL AMONG THIEVES?

GO THEN, AND LIVE YOUR LIVES DOING THE SAME AS THE GOOD MAN FROM SAMARIA.

THE GREAT
LESSONS

THE NEW DOC-TRINE

HEARS MY WORDS AND

WHOEVER

ACTS UPON THEM IS WISE, AND BUILDS ON A FOUNDATION MADE OF STONE.

THE RAINS DESCEND, AND THE FLOODS RISE. HURRICANE WINDS BEAT AGAINST THE HOUSE, YET IT STANDS STRONG: FOR IT IS BUILT ON SOLID ROCK.

BUT WHOEVER HEARS MY LIFE-GIVING WORDS AND REJECTS THEM CHOOSES TO BUILD ON A FOUNDATION OF SAND. THE RAINS DESCEND, AND THE FLOODS RISE. HURRICANE WINDS BEAT AGAINST THE HOUSE, AND THE FOUNDATION CRUMBLES. THE HOUSE COLLAPSES, AND GREAT IS ITS FALL.

ONCE, THERE WERE TWO MEN WHO WENT INTO THE TEMPLE TO PRAY. ONE WAS A PROUD, SELF-RIGHTEOUS MAN, WHILE THE OTHER WAS A MISERABLE TAX COLLECTOR WELL KNOWN FOR HIS DISHONESTY. THE PROUD MAN PRAYED: "THANK GOD I AM NOT A SINNER LIKE OTHER PEOPLE, ESPECIALLY THAT CHEATING TAX COLLECTOR I SEE HERE TODAY. I NEVER CHEAT, NOR DO I COMMIT

ADULTERY. I FAST TWICE A WEEK, AND I GIVE THE TEMPLE A TENTH OF ALL THAT I EARN."

THE TAX COLLECTOR REMAINED IN THE BACK OF THE TEMPLE, AND DARED NOT LIFT HIS EYES TOWARD HEAVEN. HE PRAYED SORROWFULLY: "GOD, PLEASE BE MERCIFUL TO ME. I AM UNWORTHY AND HAVE FALLEN SHORT OF WHAT YOU ASK."

I TELL YOU NOW THAT THE TAX COLLECTOR WHO RECOGNIZED HIS NEED FOR GOD'S MERCY RETURNED TO HIS HOUSE LIGHTHEARTED, FREE FROM ANXIETY, AND FORGIVEN. THOSE WHO, IN THEIR PRIDE, EXALT THEMSELVES WILL BE HUMBLED, WHILE THOSE WHO HUMBLE THEMSELVES WILL RISE ABOVE THE CARES OF THIS WORLD TO A PLACE OF BLESSING AND HONOR.

LET THE LITTLE CHILDREN COME TO ME, AND DO NOT REFUSE THEM. THE KINGDOM OF GOD BELONGS TO HEARTS SO TRUSTING; FOR WITHOUT A CHILDLIKE FAITH, YOU WILL NEVER ENTER THE KINGDOM.

MY DOCTRINE IS NOT MY OWN, BUT HIS WHO HAS SENT ME. IF YOU CHOOSE TO DO MY FATHER'S WILL, YOU WILL QUICKLY DISCOVER WHETHER OR NOT MY TEACHING COMES FROM GOD.

THE WORLD WORSHIPS BLINDLY. AT LEAST AS JEWS WE KNOW WHAT WE WORSHIP, AND THAT THE WORLD'S SALVATION IS BORN FROM AMONG US. BELIEVE ME: THE TIME IS COMING, AND HAS ALREADY COME, WHEN THOSE WHO WOULD WORSHIP GOD WILL CEASE FROM THEIR CONSTANT SEARCHING. NO LONGER WILL PEOPLE SEARCH FOR THE DWELLING PLACE OF GOD, ANNOUNCING: "HERE IT IS! THIS IS WHERE WE SHOULD PRAY."

NO, TRUE BELIEVERS WILL WORSHIP GOD IN SPIRIT AND TRUTH, AND GOD THE FATHER WILL SEEK OUT THOSE WHO APPROACH HIM OFFERING THE SACRIFICE OF WORSHIP AND PRAISE. IF YOU KEEP SILENT YOUR PRAISE, THE VERY STONES AT YOUR FEET WILL CRY OUT.

PERHAPS YOU HAVE READ THAT WHEN KING DAVID AND HIS SOLDIERS WERE HUNGRY, THEY ENTERED THE TEMPLE AND ATE FROM THE HOLY BREAD NORMALLY RESERVED FOR THE PRIESTS. THIS WAS AN ACT CLEARLY FORBIDDEN BY THE RELIGIOUS LAWS. AND YET, IF YOU WERE AN OBSERVER OF THE HEBREW LAWS, YOU WOULD KNOW THAT ON THE SABBATH DAYS THE PRIESTS THAT WORK IN THE TEMPLE DESECRATE THE SABBATH BY THEIR LABOR, YET ARE COUNTED BLAMELESS.

ARE THERE NOT MORE IMPORTANT THINGS THAN THE LAWS OF THE TEMPLE? UNDERSTAND THEN, THE MEANING OF THE SCRIPTURE, "I PREFER MERCY TO SACRIFICE." BY SO DOING, YOU WILL CEASE FROM YOUR CONDEMNATION OF THE GUILTLESS. THE SON OF MAN IS LORD EVEN OF THE SABBATH DAY.

SUPPOSE AN ANIMAL IN YOUR CARE FELL INTO A DITCH ON THE SABBATH, WOULD NOT YOU MAKE EVERY EFFORT TO FREE IT? IS NOT YOUR LIFE EQUALLY VALUABLE? YOU THINK NOTHING

OF SPENDING THE SABBATH OBSERVING THE CEREMONY OF RELIGION OR PRACTICING LONG LITURGIES, HOW IS IT THEN THAT YOU CRITICIZE ME FOR HEALING ON THE LORD'S DAY? WHEN WILL YOU STOP JUDGING BY OUTWARD APPEARANCES AND BEGIN TO MAKE RIGHT YOUR JUDGMENTS? THE SABBATH WAS CREATED FOR YOU. YOU WERE NOT CREATED FOR THE SABBATH.

I HAVE COME INTO THIS WORLD THAT THE BLIND MIGHT SEE, AND THEY THAT BOAST OF THEIR VISION MIGHT BECOME AWARE OF THE BLINDNESS THAT HAS BEFALLEN THEM.
"TRUE BELIEVERS WILL WORSHIP GOD
IN
SPIRIT AND TRUTH."

THE BLESS- INGS

BLESSED ARE YOU WHO HEAR THE WORD OF GOD AND

FOLLOW IT WHERE IT LEADS. IN DOING SO, YOU WILL BE LIKE THE SERVANT WHO, WHEN THE MASTER COMES, IS FOUND DOING RIGHT.

BLESSED ARE YOU, WHO PUT YOUR WHOLE TRUST IN GOD. YOURS IS THE KINGDOM OF HEAVEN. BLESSED ARE YOU, WHO ARE ACQUAINTED WITH SORROW, FOR YOU WILL BE APPOINTED GREAT COMFORT AND COURAGE. BLESSED ARE YOU, WHO WITH HUMILITY RECOGNIZE YOUR NEED OF GOD. THE WHOLE EARTH WILL BE YOURS. BLESSED ARE YOU, WHO HUNGER AND THIRST AFTER RIGHTEOUSNESS. YOU WILL BE SATISFIED AND FILLED. BLESSED ARE YOU, WHO ARE MERCIFUL. YOU WILL RECEIVE MERCY IN RETURN. BLESSED ARE YOU, WHO ARE PURE IN HEART. YOU WILL SEE GOD.

BLESSED ARE YOU PEACEMAKERS, FOR YOU WILL BE CALLED THE CHILDREN OF GOD. BLESSED ARE YOU, WHO PURSUE SALVATION. YOU WILL BECOME THE CITIZENS OF THE KINGDOM OF GOD. BLESSED ARE YOU WHEN YOU SUFFER BLAME AND ARE SPOKEN OF EVILLY FOR DOING MY WILL. REJOICE! LEAP FOR JOY! GREAT IS YOUR REWARD IN HEAVEN. IN A SIMILAR MANNER, THEY PERSECUTED THE PROPHETS BEFORE YOUR TIME.

THE POW-
ER OF
PRAYER

UNTIL NOW, YOU HAVE ASKED
NOTHING IN MY NAME. ASK,
AND

YOU WILL RECEIVE, AND YOUR JOY WILL BE FULL.

ONCE, A MAN APPEARED AT HIS FRIEND'S DOOR AFTER MIDNIGHT. "LEND ME THREE LOAVES OF BREAD," HE CALLED. "I HAVE VISITORS WHO HAVE TRAVELED FAR TO SEE ME, AND MY CUPBOARDS ARE BARE."

BUT HIS FRIEND REPLIED: "PLEASE DON'T DISTURB ME NOW. THE DOOR IS LOCKED, AND MY CHILDREN ARE ASLEEP. I CAN'T GET UP AND HELP YOU."

HERE IS A LESSON. THOUGH THE MAN DID NOT GET UP AND PROVIDE THE BREAD BECAUSE OF THEIR FRIENDSHIP, HE DID EVENTUALLY GIVE IN TO HIS FRIEND'S EARNEST PLEADING, AND ROSE FROM HIS SLEEP TO GIVE HIM WHAT HE ASKED.

BE SO PERSISTENT IN YOUR REQUESTS TO GOD. ASK, AND IT WILL BE GIVEN TO YOU. SEEK, AND YOU WILL FIND. KNOCK, AND THE DOOR WILL BE OPENED TO YOU. FOR EVERYONE WHO ASKS RECEIVES, THOSE WHO SEEK FIND, AND TO THOSE WHO KNOCK, THE DOOR WILL BE OPENED WIDE.

IN A CERTAIN TOWN, THERE LIVED A HARD-HEARTED JUDGE, WHO NEITHER FEARED GOD NOR CARED FOR HIS NEIGHBOR. IN THE SAME TOWN THERE LIVED A

WIDOW, WHO PURSUED HIM FOR JUSTICE CONCERNING A PERSON WHO HAD HARMED HER. TIME PASSED, AND THE JUDGE PERSISTED IN IGNORING HER PLEAS, REFUSING TO HEAR HER CASE, UNTIL FINALLY, ONE DAY, HE SAID TO HIMSELF:

"THOUGH I DO NOT FEAR GOD, NOR CONCERN MYSELF WITH CHARITY, I WILL SEE TO IT THAT THIS WIDOW GETS JUSTICE; FOR SHE WEARS ME OUT WITH HER CONSTANT APPEALS."

WILL NOT GOD THEN OFFER JUSTICE TO HIS CHOSEN ONES, WHO CRY OUT TO HIM DAY AND NIGHT? WILL HE TOO IGNORE YOUR EARNEST CRY FOR HELP? I TELL YOU THIS: HE WILL SEE THAT THEY WHO SEEK HIM RECEIVE JUSTICE, AND QUICKLY! AND YET, THE REAL QUESTION RAISED IN THIS STORY IS THIS: WHEN THE MESSIAH RETURNS, WILL HE FIND MANY ON THE EARTH WITH SUCH PERSEVERING FAITH?

I DO NOT MEAN THAT YOU SHOULD LET YOUR PRAYER FALL INTO A PATTERN OF MINDLESS REPETITION. THE UNENLIGHTENED PRAY IN THIS MANNER, IMAGINING THAT THEY WILL BE HEARD BECAUSE OF THE GREAT NUMBER OF THEIR PRAYERS. DO NOT IMITATE THEM. REMEMBER: YOUR HEAVENLY FATHER KNOWS WHAT YOU NEED EVEN BEFORE YOU ASK.

THE PROPHET ISAIAH HAS WRITTEN: "MY HOUSE SHALL BE CALLED BY ALL NATIONS A HOUSE OF PRAYER."

PRAY THEN, TO THE FATHER WHO HEARS YOUR MOST INTIMATE PRAYERS AND REWARDS THEM OPENLY; AND WHATEVER YOU ASK THE FATHER IN MY NAME, HE WILL PROVIDE. IF YOU LIVE YOUR LIFE IN ME, AND LET MY WORDS LIVE IN YOU, YOU MAY ASK WHAT YOU WISH AND IT WILL BE GIVEN TO YOU.

PRAY IN THIS MANNER:

"OUR FATHER IN HEAVEN, MAY ALL THE EARTH RECOGNIZE THAT YOU ARE THE ONE AND HOLY GOD.

MAY YOUR KINGDOM DWELL AMONG US. MAY YOUR PURPOSE BE ACCOMPLISHED ON EARTH, AS IT IS IN HEAVEN. PROVIDE US WITH DAILY BREAD TO SUSTAIN US, AND FORGIVE OUR FALLING SHORT. HELP US TO FORGIVE THOSE WHO HAVE WRONGED US. KEEP US FROM WANDERING INTO FAITHLESSNESS, AND DELIVER US FROM THE EVIL ONE. FOR TO YOU BELONGS ALL POWER AND GLORY, ETERNALLY. LET IT BE SO."

REMEMBER: YOUR HEAVENLY FATHER KNOWS WHAT YOU NEED EVEN BEFORE YOU ASK."

THE TREA-SURES IN HEAVEN

LIVE YOUR LIVES
DOING TO

OTHERS AS YOU WOULD HAVE THEM DO TO YOU.

ONCE THERE WAS A RICH MAN WHO DRESSED IN PURPLE AND FINE LINEN, ENJOYING A LIFE OF EXTRAVAGANCE. IN THE SAME TOWN THERE LIVED A HOMELESS MAN NAMED LAZARUS, WHO SAT NEAR THE GATE THAT LED TO THE RICH MAN'S HOUSE. HE DID NOT ASK FOR ANYTHING BUT THE CRUMBS THAT FELL FROM THE RICH MAN'S TABLE. STRAY DOGS WERE HIS ONLY FRIENDS, AND THEY LICKED HIS WOUNDS.

FINALLY, ONE DAY LAZARUS DIED AND WAS CARRIED BY ANGELS INTO THE ARMS OF ABRAHAM. NOT LONG AFTERWARDS, THE RICH MAN ALSO DIED, AND WAS BURIED.

FROM THE AGONIES OF HELL HE LIFTED HIS EYES FULL OF TORMENT, AND SEEING ABRAHAM A GREAT WAY OFF, HE CRIED: "FATHER ABRAHAM, HAVE MERCY UPON ME, AND SEND THE BEGGAR LAZARUS TO COMFORT ME! HAVE HIM DIP THE TIP OF HIS FINGER IN WATER TO COOL MY TONGUE, FOR I SUFFER HERE IN THESE FLAMES!"

BUT ABRAHAM REPLIED: "MY SON, REMEMBER THAT IN YOUR LIFETIME YOU ENJOYED YOUR GOOD THINGS, WHILE LAZARUS KNEW ONLY SUFFERING AND MISERY. NOW, HE IS COMFORTED, AND YOU ARE THE ONE TORMENTED. BESIDES, BETWEEN US IS FIXED A GREAT GULF OF SEPARATION, SO THAT THOSE WHO WOULD COME TO YOU FROM HERE CANNOT, NEITHER CAN YOU, CROSS OVER TO US FROM WHERE YOU SUFFER."

HEARING THESE WORDS, THE RICH MAN CRIED OUT: "I PRAY, THEN, THAT YOU SEND LAZARUS TO MY FATHER'S HOUSE. I HAVE FIVE BROTHERS, AND HE MUST WARN THEM, SO THEY DO NOT END UP IN THIS HELL."

TO THIS, ABRAHAM ANSWERED: "THEY HAVE MOSES AND THE PROPHETS. LET THEM HEAR THEM."

"BUT SURELY," THE RICH MAN PROTESTED, "IF ONE WERE TO APPEAR TO THEM FROM THE DEAD, THEY WOULD REPENT."

ABRAHAM REPLIED: "IF THEY DO NOT REPENT BECAUSE OF THE WORDS OF MOSES AND THE

PROPHETS, THEY WILL NOT BE PERSUADED, EVEN IF ONE SHOULD APPEAR TO THEM FROM THE DEAD."

THERE IS NO GENEROSITY IN GIVING TO THOSE WHO CAN EASILY REPAY. EVEN MISERS LEND MONEY WHEN THEY ARE CERTAIN OF BEING REPAID IN FULL. GIVE TO THOSE WHO APPEAR BEFORE YOU IN NEED, TO THE DESTITUTE WITH NO HOPE OF REPAYING YOUR GIFT. PRACTICE FORGIVENESS, EVEN IF SUCH PERSONS TAKE ADVANTAGE OF YOUR KIND ACTS.

THE POOR, WHEN THEY GIVE, CONTRIBUTE MORE THAN THE WEALTHY, WHO GIVE FROM THEIR ABUNDANCE. THE POOR CONTRIBUTE FROM THEIR NEED, AND WITH GREAT LOVE OFTEN GIVE WHAT THEY CANNOT SPARE.

HOW NEARLY IMPOSSIBLE IT IS FOR THOSE WHO LOVE MONEY TO ENTER THE KINGDOM OF GOD! IT IS EASIER FOR A CAMEL TO SQUEEZE THROUGH THE EYE OF A NEEDLE THAN FOR A RICH MAN TO ENTER INTO THE KINGDOM. AND YET, WHAT IS IMPOSSIBLE FOR MAN IS MADE POSSIBLE BY GOD'S MERCY.

DO NOT HOARD TREASURES ON EARTH WHERE MOTHS

AND RUST CORRUPT, AND WHERE THIEVES BREAK IN AND STEAL. STORE YOUR TREASURES IN HEAVEN, WHERE NEITHER MOTHS NOR RUST CORRUPT, NOR THIEVES BREAK IN TO STEAL. WHERE YOUR TREASURE IS, THERE YOU HEART WILL ALSO BE.

SOME DO GOOD ACTS ONLY WHEN THEY ARE CERTAIN OF AN AUDIENCE. FOR THESE, THERE IS NO REWARD. WHEN YOU GIVE, DO NOT BEHAVE LIKE THE HYPOCRITES, WHO RING BELLS IN THE TEMPLE AND PARADE IN THE STREETS. THESE HAVE THEIR OWN REWARD.

DO NOT EVEN LET YOUR LEFT HAND KNOW WHAT YOUR RIGHT HAND IS DOING. GIVE QUIETLY AND IN SECRET; AND YOUR HEAVENLY FATHER WHO SEES SUCH ACTS OF KINDNESS WILL REWARD YOU OPENLY.

LEARN TO GIVE AND IT WILL BE GIVEN BACK TO YOU ABUNDANTLY, MORE THAN YOU CAN IMAGINE, MULTIPLIED AND OVERFLOWING. BY THE SAME MEASURE THAT YOU DISTRIBUTE YOUR GENEROSITY, YOUR REWARD WILL BE MEASURED IN RETURN.

ONCE, THE INVESTMENT OF A RICH MAN YIELDED A GREAT PROFIT. CONSIDERING HIS INCREASED RICHES, THE MAN SAID TO HIMSELF, "WHAT SHALL I DO WITH MY PROFITS?" AND HE CAME TO THIS DECISION: "I WILL PULL DOWN MY OLD HOUSES, AND BUILD ONES THAT ARE GREATER. I HAVE AMASSED IMMENSE TREASURE, AND WILL REJOICE IN MY WEALTH. I WILL BE CONTENT FOR MANY YEARS TO COME, AND WILL SPEND MY TIME EATING, DRINKING, AND BEING MERRY."

BUT GOD SAID TO HIM: "RECKLESS MAN! DO YOU NOT KNOW THAT THIS SAME NIGHT YOUR SOUL WILL BE DEMANDED OF YOU! WHEN YOU ARE GONE, WHOSE WILL ALL THESE THINGS BE?"

SUCH IS THE FATE OF THOSE WHO STORE UP TREASURE FOR THEMSELVES, AND ARE NOT RICH IN THE POSSESSIONS OF GOD. WHAT MERIT IS THERE IN ATTAINING ALL THAT THE WORLD CAN OFFER, IF IN SO DOING YOU FORFEIT YOUR SOUL? WHAT CAN BE GIVEN IN EXCHANGE FOR YOUR SOUL, OR YOUR PLACE IN THE KINGDOM OF HEAVEN?

FAITH THAT MOVES MOUN- TAINS

ACCORDING TO YOUR   FAITH,

SO YOU WILL RECEIVE.

MANY WILL COME IN THE LAST DAYS, FROM EVERY CORNER OF THE EARTH, AND ENTER INTO THE KINGDOM OF HEAVEN. BUT THE SELF-RIGHTEOUS AND PIOUS, WHO THOUGHT THEY WOULD BE FIRST, AND YET LIVED THEIR LIVES WITHOUT FAITH, WILL NOT ENTER IN.

IF TWO AGREE BY FAITH, MY FATHER IN HEAVEN WILL GRANT THEIR REQUEST. FOR WHEREVER TWO OR THREE ARE GATHERED IN MY NAME, I AM PRESENT WITH THEM.

THESE SIGNS WILL FOLLOW THOSE WHO BELIEVE: IN MY NAME THEY WILL CAST OUT DEVILS. THEY WILL SPEAK WITH NEW TONGUES. SERPENTS, OR DEADLY THINGS, WILL NOT HARM THEM. THEY WILL LAY HANDS ON THE SICK, AND THE SICK WILL BE MADE WHOLE.

POSSESSING FAITH THE SIZE OF A MUSTARD SEED, THEY SHALL SAY TO THE MOUNTAINS: "BE REMOVED AND CAST INTO THE SEA."

IF YOU BELIEVE ALL THINGS TO BE POSSIBLE AND LEAVE NO ROOM FOR DOUBT, WHAT YOU ASK OR COMMAND WILL BE DONE. THIS IS WHY I TELL YOU: WHATEVER IT IS THAT YOU DESIRE, WHEN YOU PRAY, BELIEVE THAT YOU WILL RECEIVE IT, AND YOU WILL.

AS YOU LIVE YOUR LIFE INVIGORATED BY THE BREATH OF GOD, THE CONFLICTS OF THIS EARTH WILL BE OVERCOME BY HEAVEN'S POWER: AND WHATEVER YOU ALLOCATE ON EARTH WILL BE THAT WHICH IS IN ACCORDANCE TO HEAVEN'S PLAN.

DO NOT BE AFRAID ANY LONGER, BUT BELIEVE. EVERYTHING IS POSSIBLE TO THE ONE WHO BELIEVES.

"EVERYTHING IS POSSIBLE TO
THE ONE WHO BELIEVES.

PATIENCE, MERCY AND FOR-GIVENESS

WHEN LITTLE IS FORGIVEN,

LITTLE LOVE IS RETURNED.

A CERTAIN MAN WAS REVIEWING THE ACCOUNTS OF TWO MEN WHO HAD BORROWED MONEY.

ONE OWED HIM FIVE HUNDRED GOLD PIECES, WHILE THE OTHER OWED HIM FIFTY. KNOWING THAT NEITHER HAD ANY MEANS OF REPAYING HIM, HE COMPASSIONATELY FORGAVE BOTH OF THEIR DEBTS. WHICH OF THESE TWO MEN DO YOU SUPPOSE WAS THE MOST GRATEFUL?

LIKEWISE, THE TIME CAME FOR A CERTAIN KING TO APPRAISE HIS FINANCIAL RECORDS. DURING THIS PROCESS, ONE OF HIS SERVANTS, WHO OWED A STAGGERING AMOUNT OF TEN THOUSAND GOLD PIECES, WAS BROUGHT BEFORE HIM.

SINCE IT WAS IMPOSSIBLE THAT THE SERVANT EVER REPAY SUCH A DEBT, THE KING RESORTED TO THE LAW, WHICH DECREED THAT THE DEBTOR AND HIS FAMILY BE SOLD INTO SLAVERY, AND THEIR HOUSE AND POSSESSIONS BE DISPOSED OF IN A PUBLIC AUCTION.

SORROWFULLY, THE SERVANT FELL TO HIS KNEES BEFORE THE KING AND CRIED: "MY LORD AND KING, I BEG YOU TO HAVE PATIENCE WITH ME, AND I WILL REPAY YOU ALL THAT I OWE."

SO MOVED WAS THE KING WITH COMPASSION THAT HE FORGAVE THE DEBT, AND LET HIS SERVANT GO FREE.

ON HIS WAY HOME, THIS SAME SERVANT ENCOUNTERED A FRIEND WHO OWED HIM A FEW PENNIES. INSTEAD OF SHOWING MERCY, HOWEVER, HE SEIZED THE MAN BY THE THROAT, SHOUTING: "THIEF! PAY ME BACK THE COINS THAT YOU BORROWED FROM ME."

HIS FRIEND FELL AT HIS FEET AND PLEADED: "PLEASE BE PATIENT! I SWEAR THAT I WILL REPAY YOU EVERY LAST CENT."

BUT THE SERVANT WOULDN'T LISTEN, EVEN TO HIS FRIEND'S BEGGING AND TEARS, AND HAD THE POOR MAN DRAGGED OFF TO PRISON UNTIL HE COULD REPAY THE DEBT ACCORDING TO THE LAW.

BY CHANCE, SOME OF THE KING'S SERVANTS WITNESSED THIS OUTRAGEOUS BEHAVIOR AND REPORTED IT BACK TO THE KING.

IMMEDIATELY, THE KING SENT FOR HIS SERVANT AND SAID: "WICKED SERVANT. I FORGAVE YOU AN IMMENSE DEBT SIMPLY OUT OF MERCY. COULDN'T YOU HAVE SHOWN SIMILAR COMPASSION TO YOUR OWN FRIEND WHO OWED YOU SUCH AN INSIGNIFICANT SUM?"

HAVING SAID THIS, THE KING HANDED THE SERVANT OVER TO HIS PRISON GUARDS, AND COMMANDED THEM TO LOCK HIM AWAY UNTIL ALL HIS DEBTS HAD BEEN PAID. SO WILL MY HEAVENLY FATHER JUDGE YOU IF YOU REFUSE TO FORGIVE YOUR OWN BROTHERS AND SISTERS FROM THE DEPTHS OF YOUR HEARTS.

DO NOT LIMIT YOUR ATTITUDE OF FORGIVENESS. ARE YOU WILLING TO FORGIVE SEVEN TIMES? SEVENTY TIMES SEVEN TIMES IS MORE APPROPRIATE. MAKE PEACE, EVEN WITH YOUR ENEMIES. CONSTANT

STRIVING WILL LEAD ONLY TO GREATER TROUBLE: LAWSUITS, COURTROOMS, EVEN PRISON, WITH NO WAY OF UNDOING THE PENALTY EXCEPT BY COMPLETING YOUR SENTENCE.

DO YOU REMEMBER THE SAYING: AN EYE FOR AN EYE, AND A TOOTH FOR A TOOTH? I TELL YOU THE OPPOSITE. IF SOMEBODY STRIKES YOU ON THE RIGHT CHEEK, OFFER HIM YOUR LEFT; OR IF SOMEONE SUES YOU AND TAKES YOUR COAT, OFFER THE SHIRT OFF YOUR BACK AS WELL. IF SOMEONE COMPELS YOU TO WALK ONE MILE, BE WILLING TO WALK TWO. GIVE FREELY TO THOSE WHO ASK OF YOU, AND NEVER TURN A DEAF EAR TO THOSE IN NEED.

WHEN YOU STAND IN THE PLACE OF WORSHIP, DO SO WITH A HEART OVERFLOWING WITH FORGIVENESS, EVEN AS YOUR FATHER IN HEAVEN FORGIVES YOU. AND SHOULD YOU BRING AN OFFERING INTO THE PLACE OF WORSHIP, ONLY THEN REMEMBERING AN UNRESOLVED DISAGREEMENT, LEAVE YOUR GIFT AT THE ALTAR. GO FIRST AND BE RECONCILED, AND THEN

RETURN TO MAKE AN OFFERING OF YOUR GIFT. IF SOMEONE WRONGS YOU, GO AND DISCUSS IT WITH THAT PERSON IN PRIVATE. IF THEY LISTEN TO YOU, YOU WILL HAVE GAINED A FRIEND.

LEARN TO PRACTICE FORGIVENESS, AND YOUR LIFE WILL BE FILLED WITH MERCY AND GRACE. "GIVE FREELY TO THOSE WHO ASK OF YOU, AND NEVER TURN A DEAF EAR TO THOSE IN NEED."

ON A FRUITFUL LIFE

THE FRUIT OF PEOPLE'S LIVES WILL REVEAL

THE LIFE THEY HAVE CHOSEN TO LIVE.

YOU ARE THE SALT OF THE EARTH. BUT IF THE SALT HAS LOST ITS POWER TO PURIFY, FLAVOR, AND PRESERVE, HOW CAN IT BE MADE SALT AGAIN? IT IS WORTHLESS, EXCEPT TO BE DISCARDED AND TRAMPLED UNDER FOOT.

DO YOU PICK GRAPES FROM THORN BUSHES, OR FIGS FROM AMONG THISTLES? A HEALTHY TREE CANNOT PRODUCE UNHEALTHY FRUIT; NOR DOES A ROTTEN TREE PRODUCE HEALTHY FRUIT. LIKEWISE, EVERY GOOD TREE PRODUCES GOOD FRUIT, AND EVERY ROTTEN TREE PRODUCES ROTTEN FRUIT. THE UNHEALTHY TREE IS CUT DOWN AND USED AS WOOD FOR THE FIRE.

ONCE, A MAN PLANTED A FIG TREE WITHIN THE WALLS OF HIS VINEYARD. FOR THREE YEARS HE WAITED FOR IT TO BEAR FRUIT, BUT NONE CAME. AT LAST HE CALLED THE CHIEF GARDENER: "THREE YEARS I HAVE WALKED HERE, EACH YEAR EXPECTING TO FIND FRUIT FROM THIS FIG TREE; AND STILL IT IS BARREN. WHY SHOULD IT TAKE UP SPACE ON MY GROUNDS ANY LONGER? CUT IT DOWN."

TO THIS, THE GARDENER REPLIED: "GIVE THE TREE ONE MORE SEASON. I WILL FERTILIZE ITS ROOTS

AND GIVE IT SPECIAL ATTENTION. PERHAPS THEN, IT WILL BEAR FRUIT. IF NOT, YOU DO RIGHT IN CUTTING IT DOWN."

WHEN YOUR LIVES BEAR FRUIT, MY FATHER IS GLORIFIED, AND YOU BECOME MY TRUE DISCIPLES. FROM A GOOD LIFE FLOWS GOODNESS FROM WHAT IS STORED WITHIN; WHILE AN EVIL LIFE PRODUCES ONLY BARRENNESS.

A FARMER WENT INTO THE FIELD TO SOW. AS HE SOWED, SOME SEEDS FELL BY THE ROADSIDE AND THE BIRDS SWARMED DOWN AND ATE THEM. SOME OF THE SEEDS FELL AMONG STONY PLACES, WHERE THERE WAS NOT ENOUGH EARTH. HERE, THEY SPROUTED QUICKLY IN THE SHALLOW SOIL BUT LACKING ROOTS, WERE SCORCHED BY THE SUN AND SOON WITHERED. SOME SEEDS FELL AMONG BRAMBLE BUSHES AND WERE CHOKED BY THE THORNS.

BUT CERTAIN OF THESE SEEDS DID FIND GOOD EARTH, AND THESE MADE UP FOR THE SEEDS THAT WERE LOST AND YIELDED A GOOD CROP; RETURNING A HARVEST THAT WAS THIRTY, SIXTY, AND EVEN ONE HUNDRED TIMES THE SEED THAT WAS PLANTED.

WHEN YOU HEAR THE WORD OF THE KINGDOM AND FAIL TO UNDERSTAND THE TEACHING, THE ENEMY COMES AND STEALS AWAY THE SEED THAT IS PLANTED IN THE HEART. THIS IS SIMILAR TO THE SEED THAT FELL BY THE ROADSIDE.

THE SEED THAT WAS SCATTERED ON STONY GROUND REPRESENTS THOSE WHO HEAR THE WORD OF GOD AND EAGERLY ACCEPT IT, BUT HAVE NO ROOTS OF INNER CONVICTION. THEIR EXPERIENCE MIGHT LAST FOR A TIME, BUT WHEN TROUBLE OR PERSECUTION ARISES RESULTING FROM THEIR DECISION TO FOLLOW THE TRUTH, THEY BECOME DISCOURAGED AND DRIFT AWAY.

THE SEED THAT WAS SOWN AMONG THE THORN BUSHES REPRESENTS THOSE THAT HEAR THESE WORDS, BUT ARE SOON OVERWHELMED BY THE CARES OF THIS WORLD AND THE DECEITFULNESS OF RICHES. THE TEACHING IS CHOKED, AND THEIR LIVES BECOME BARREN.

THE SEED THAT FELL ON GOOD EARTH REPRESENTS THOSE THAT HEAR THESE WORDS AND UNDERSTAND THE MESSAGE THEY CONTAIN. THEIR LIVES WILL YIELD ACCORDINGLY AN ABUNDANT HARVEST: THIRTY, SIXTY, AND ONE HUNDRED TIMES THE GOOD THAT IS PLANTED WITHIN.

HEALTH AND HEALING FOR BODY AND SOUL

THOSE THAT ARE HEALTHY DO NOT NEED A DOCTOR; BUT THOSE THAT ARE ILL ARE IN NEED OF ONE.

YOU SHOULD UNDERSTAND THIS: I DESIRE MERCY, NOT SACRIFICE. FOR I HAVE NOT COME TO CALL THE RIGHTEOUS BUT THE LOST TO REPENTANCE. SHOULDN'T THE SICK IN BODY, WHO THE DEVIL HAS BOUND, BE SET FREE?

IS IT EASIER TO SAY "YOUR SINS ARE FORGIVEN," OR "RISE AND BE HEALED"?

THAT YOU MIGHT KNOW BEYOND THE SHADOW OF A DOUBT THAT THE SON OF MAN HAS POWER ON EARTH TO FORGIVE ALL WRONGS, I ANNOUNCE TO THE SICK: "RISE UP! BE OF GOOD CHEER; YOUR WRONGS ARE FORGIVEN. GO YOUR WAY! AS YOU HAVE BELIEVED, SO SHALL YOU RECEIVE. YOUR FAITH HAS MADE YOU WELL!"

WHILE COUNTING HIS FLOCK OF ONE HUNDRED SHEEP, A SHEPHERD DISCOVERED ONE MISSING.

IMMEDIATELY, HE LEFT THE NINETY-NINE IN THE SAFETY OF THE FOLD, AND WENT IN SEARCH OF THE ONE THAT WAS LOST. AND WHEN THE LOST SHEEP WAS FOUND, HE CARRIED IT HOME IN HIS ARMS, HIS HEART FILLED WITH GLADNESS. ON THE WAY, HE CALLED OUT TO HIS FRIENDS AND ANYONE WHO WOULD LISTEN, "REJOICE WITH ME! THIS, MY LOST SHEEP, HAS BEEN FOUND."

I TELL YOU THIS TRUTH: THERE IS MORE REJOICING IN HEAVEN OVER ONE WHO REPENTS, THAN OVER NINETY-NINE WHO NEED NO REPENTANCE.

WHO AMONG YOU, HAVING TEN PIECES OF SILVER AND LOSING ONE PIECE,

WOULD NOT LIGHT A CANDLE, AND CAREFULLY
SWEEP THE HOUSE, SEARCHING DILIGENTLY UNTIL
IT IS FOUND?

WHEN THE COIN IS FOUND AT LAST, DO YOU NOT
CALL YOUR FRIENDS AND NEIGHBORS, SAYING: "GOOD
NEWS! I FOUND THE MONEY THAT WAS LOST."

LIKEWISE, I TELL YOU, THERE IS GREAT JOY IN
THE PRESENCE OF THE FATHER AND ALL OF THE
ANGELS, WHEN ONE TURNS FROM THEIR PATH
OF WRONGDOING.

THE CALL TO A NEW LIFE

THE CALL

YOU HAVE NOT
CHOSEN ME.

I HAVE CHOSEN YOU, AND APPOINTED YOU TO PRODUCE GOOD FRUIT FROM THE LIVES THAT YOU LIVE, FRUIT THAT WILL LAST.

A MAN HAD TWO SONS. HE SAID TO THE ELDER: "SON, GO AND WORK TODAY IN MY VINEYARD."

"I WILL NOT," THE SON REPLIED; BUT LATER HE EXPERIENCED A CHANGE OF HEART, AND WENT TO THE FIELDS TO WORK.

THEN THE FATHER SAID TO THE YOUNGER SON: "GO INTO THE FIELDS AS WELL."

IMMEDIATELY HE ANSWERED: "I WILL." BUT HE REMAINED AT HOME, AND IGNORED HIS FATHER'S WORDS. WHICH OF THESE TWO SONS FULFILLED THEIR FATHER'S REQUEST?

WHY DO YOU CALL ME GOOD, UNLESS YOU BELIEVE I AM GOD? YOU KNOW THE COMMANDMENTS: DO NOT COMMIT ADULTERY; DO NOT KILL; DO NOT STEAL; DO NOT BEAR FALSE WITNESS; HONOR YOUR FATHER AND YOUR MOTHER. DOING THIS, YOU WILL HAVE TREASURES IN HEAVEN. AND YET, YOU FALL SHORT

BY HONORING ME WITH YOUR WORDS ALONE, AND NOT USING EVERYTHING — YOUR WEALTH, YOUR POSSESSIONS, AND YOUR LIFE — TO HELP THOSE IN NEED.

IF YOU WISH TO FOLLOW ME, YOU MUST FIRST PUT ASIDE YOUR OWN DESIRES AND YOUR SELF-CENTERED WAYS. SACRIFICE YOUR PRIDE AND FOLLOW ME. THOSE WHO DESIRE ETERNAL LIFE MUST PUT ASIDE THEIR OLD WAY OF LIFE. ALL WHO DO THIS FOR MY SAKE WILL DISCOVER NEW LIFE — BOTH HERE ON EARTH AS WELL AS IN HEAVEN.

ONCE THERE WAS A KING WHO PLANNED THE WEDDING OF HIS SON. WHEN ALL WAS READY, HE SENT FORTH HIS SERVANTS TO THE PROVINCES OF HIS KINGDOM TO SUMMON THOSE INVITED TO THE WEDDING. INCREDIBLY, THE GUESTS REFUSED TO COME.

UNDAUNTED, THE KING SENT OUT HIS SERVANTS A SECOND TIME, SAYING: "TELL THOSE INVITED TO THE WEDDING, I HAVE PREPARED A GREAT FEAST. MY OXEN AND BEST CALVES HAVE

BEEN SLAUGHTERED, AND EVERYTHING IS READY. COME TO THE WEDDING."

BUT AGAIN THE SUBJECTS MADE LIGHT OF THE KING'S INVITATION AND RETURNED TO THEIR WORK; SOME TO THEIR FARMS, OTHERS TO THEIR SHOPS. SOME REMAINED BEHIND, AND THESE TOOK HOLD OF THE KING'S SERVANTS AND BEAT THEM TO DEATH.

WHEN THE KING LEARNED OF WHAT HAD HAPPENED, HE WAS ENRAGED. HE SENT HIS PALACE SOLDIERS INTO THE PROVINCES, AND THEY CAUGHT THE MURDERERS, EXECUTED THEM, AND BURNED THEIR HOUSES TO THE GROUND.

THEN THE KING TURNED TO HIS SERVANT. "THE WEDDING IS READY," HE SAID, "BUT THOSE WHO WERE INVITED WERE NOT WORTHY TO ATTEND. GO THEN, TO THOSE WHOM YOU MEET ON STREET CORNERS AND HIGHWAYS, AND INVITE THEM IN TO THE WEDDING."

THE SERVANTS DID AS THE KING COMMANDED THEM. THEY WENT TO THE STREET CORNERS OF THE CITY AND OUT ALONG THE HIGHWAYS AND INVITED EVERYONE THEY ENCOUNTERED, BOTH THE GOOD AND THE BAD, UNTIL THE WEDDING HALL WAS FILLED WITH GUESTS.

THAT EVENING, THE KING WAS GREATLY DISPLEASED TO SEE ONE AT THE TABLE EATING WITHOUT THE WEDDING GARMENT THAT HAD BEEN PROVIDED. HE ASKED: "HOW IS IT THAT YOU CAME IN TO THE FEAST WITHOUT YOUR WEDDING GARMENT?" BUT THE MAN COULD GIVE NO EXCUSE.

THEN THE KING SAID TO HIS SERVANTS: "BIND THIS MAN AND HAVE HIM REMOVED."

I ADD THIS TO THIS STORY: MANY ARE CALLED - INTO THE KINGDOM - BUT FEW ARE CHOSEN. THE TIME HAS COME. THE KINGDOM OF GOD IS NEAR AT HAND. I HAVE CALLED YOU FROM THE WORLD'S WAY OF LIVING. REPENT, PUT ON THE GARMENTS OF SALVATION, AND BELIEVE THIS GOOD NEWS.

NO ONE CAN COME TO ME UNLESS THE FATHER, WHO HAS SENT ME, DRAWS HIM; AND I WILL RAISE UP THAT PERSON ON THE LAST DAY. ALL OF YOU WHOM THE FATHER HAS GIVEN ME WILL COME TO ME: AND WHOEVER COMES TO ME, I WILL NEVER REFUSE.

BECAUSE I HAVE TOLD YOU SUCH THINGS, DO YOU BELIEVE? TRULY, YOU WILL WITNESS EVEN GREATER THINGS THAN THESE.

ENTER THEREFORE THROUGH THE NARROW GATE; FOR WIDE IS THE PATH, AND BROAD IS THE WAY THAT LEADS TO DESTRUCTION, AND MANY GO THAT WAY. BUT NARROW IS THE GATE AND THE PATH WHICH LEADS TO LIFE, AND THERE ARE FEW THAT FIND IT. MAKE EVERY EFFORT TO GO THROUGH THE GATE THAT LEADS TO LIFE. ONE DAY, MANY WILL WANT TO EXCHANGE THEIR WAY FOR THE RIGHT WAY, AND FIND IT TO BE TOO LATE.

ON BE-
ING BORN
A SECOND
TIME

DO NOT MARVEL WHEN

I TELL YOU THAT YOU MUST BE BORN ANEW.

TRULY, I TELL YOU: UNLESS YOU ARE BORN ANEW, YOU WILL NOT SEE THE KINGDOM OF GOD. UNLESS YOU ARE BORN OF WATER AND THE BREATH OF GOD, YOU WILL NOT ENTER INTO THE KINGDOM OF GOD.

THAT WHICH IS BORN OF THE FLESH IS FLESH; AND THAT WHICH IS BORN OF THE BREATH OF GOD IS SPIRIT. THE WIND BLOWS WHERE IT WISHES, AND WE HEAR THE SOUND THAT IT MAKES; STILL WE DO NOT KNOW FROM WHERE IT COMES, OR WHERE IT WILL GO. SO IT IS FOR THOSE WHO ARE BORN ANEW BY THE BREATH OF GOD.

CONSIDER THESE EXAMPLES: NO ONE WEAVES A PIECE OF NEW CLOTH INTO A RUINED GARMENT, FOR THE NEW PIECE WHICH IS STRONGER WILL MERELY PULL THE OLD CLOTH APART, AND THE TEAR WILL BE MADE WORSE. NEITHER DO YOU PUT NEW WINE INTO OLD WINE FLASKS, LESS THE OLD FLASKS BURST, AND THE NEW WINE SPILLS OUT, AND THE INVESTMENT BE LOST. INSTEAD YOU STORE NEW WINE IN FLASKS THAT ARE NEW, AND BOTH ARE PRESERVED.

HOW IS IT THEN THAT EVEN AFTER SO MUCH LEARNING, YOU ARE NOT FAMILIAR WITH THE MOST BASIC TRUTHS? IF I HAVE TAUGHT YOU SUCH THINGS, USING EARTHLY EXAMPLES, AND

STILL YOU FAIL TO COMPREHEND, HOW WILL YOU UNDERSTAND IF I SPEAK TO YOU OF HEAVENLY THINGS?

GOD DID NOT SEND HIS SON INTO THE WORLD TO CONDEMN THE WORLD, BUT THAT THE WORLD THROUGH HIS SON MIGHT BE REDEEMED. WHOEVER BELIEVES IN HIM IS NOT CONDEMNED; BUT WHOEVER DOES NOT BELIEVE STANDS CONDEMNED ALREADY, BECAUSE THEY HAVE NOT BELIEVED IN THE NAME OF GOD'S ONLY SON.

I AM THE RESURRECTION AND THE LIFE. WHOEVER BELIEVES IN ME, THOUGH THEY DIE ON THIS EARTH, WILL LIVE AGAIN. THEY WILL BE GIVEN ETERNAL LIFE AND NOT PERISH! I HAVE TOLD YOU MANY TIMES ALREADY: IF YOU BELIEVE, YOU WILL SEE THE GLORY OF GOD.

MY MISSION IS TO ACCOMPLISH THE PURPOSE OF HIM WHO HAS SENT ME. THIS THEN IS GOD'S WILL: THAT ALL WHO HEAR ME AND THESE WORDS COME TO TRULY BELIEVE IN THE ONE WHOM THE FATHER HAS SENT.

HEAR THIS LESSON: A MAN HAD TWO SONS. THE YOUNGER SON SAID TO HIS FATHER: "FATHER, GIVE ME MY PORTION OF THE INHERITANCE." WITHOUT QUESTIONING, THE FATHER GAVE HIM HIS SHARE.

NOT LONG AFTERWARDS THIS SAME SON GATHERED HIS POSSESSIONS, AND JOURNEYED TO A FAR COUNTRY. THERE HE SQUANDERED HIS WEALTH WITH RECKLESS LIVING. WHEN HIS LAST CENT WAS GONE, A TERRIBLE FAMINE SWEPT THE LAND, AND HE WAS LEFT DESTITUTE AND WITHOUT FRIENDS.

FINALLY HE FOUND MENIAL WORK TENDING SWINE. IN HIS DESPERATION, HE WAS ABOUT TO EAT THE CORN HUSKS RESERVED FOR THE SWINE. THEN, COMING TO HIS SENSES, HE THOUGHT: MY FATHER'S SERVANTS HAVE MORE THAN ENOUGH BREAD WITH MUCH LEFT OVER; WHILE I AM ABOUT TO EAT THE SWINE'S FOOD TO SAVE MYSELF FROM STARVATION. I WILL RETURN TO MY FATHER AND THROW MYSELF ON HIS MERCY. 'FATHER," I WILL SAY, "I HAVE WRONGED YOU AND HEAVEN, AND AM NO LONGER WORTHY TO BE YOUR SON. LET ME AT LEAST BE ONE OF YOUR HIRED SERVANTS.'"

SO DETERMINED HE ROSE FROM THE DUST, AND BEGAN THE LONG VOYAGE HOME.

WHEN HE WAS STILL A GREAT WAY OFF, HIS FATHER SAW HIM IN THE DISTANCE, AND HAVING COMPASSION ON HIM, RAN OUT TO MEET HIM AND EMBRACED HIM TENDERLY.

THE SON BEGAN HIS CONFESSION. "FATHER," HE WEPT, "I HAVE SINNED AGAINST HEAVEN AND IN YOUR SIGHT, AND AM NO

LONGER WORTHY TO BE CALLED YOUR SON."

THE FATHER DID NOT LET HIM FINISH, BUT TURNED INSTEAD TO HIS SERVANTS AND SAID: "BRING OUT MY BEST CLOTHES, AND DRESS MY SON. PUT MY SIGNET RING ON HIS HAND, AND MY FINEST SHOES ON HIS FEET. SELECT OUR FATTEST CALF FROM THE FIELD, AND PREPARE IT. LET US FEAST AND BE MERRY. FOR THIS MY SON WAS DEAD, AND IS ALIVE AGAIN; HE WAS LOST, AND NOW IS FOUND."

THEN BEGAN A GREAT CELEBRATION.

TOWARD EVENING THE ELDER BROTHER RETURNED FROM A DAY OF WORKING IN THE FIELD. AS HE DREW NEAR TO THE HOUSE, HE HEARD MUSIC AND DANCING. SUMMONING ONE OF THE SERVANTS, HE ASKED: "WHAT IS THE PURPOSE OF THIS CELEBRATION?"

THE SERVANT REPLIED: "YOUR BROTHER HAS RETURNED HOME AND YOUR FATHER HAS KILLED THE FATTEST CALF BECAUSE HE HAS RETURNED SAFE AND WITHOUT HARM."

AT THIS, THE ELDER BROTHER BECAME VERY ANGRY, AND REFUSED TO TAKE PART IN THE BANQUET. EVEN HIS FATHER BEGGED HIM TO JOIN IN THE FEASTING.

STUBBORNLY, HE REFUSED, AND SAID, "BEHOLD ALL THESE

MANY YEARS I HAVE SERVED YOU, NEVER BREAKING ONE OF YOUR COMMANDMENTS. YET YOU NEVER OFFERED ME FEASTS TO CELEBRATE WITH MY FRIENDS. NOW MY PRODIGAL BROTHER WANDERS HOME, WHO HAS NO DOUBT WASTED HIS INHERITANCE ON PROSTITUTES AND WINE, AND YOU KILL THE PRIZED CALF AND CELEBRATE!"

TO THIS, THE FATHER REPLIED: "MY SON, YOU HAVE ALWAYS BEEN FAITHFUL TO ME, AND YOU KNOW THAT ALL THAT I HAVE IS YOURS. BUT IT IS PROPER THAT WE CELEBRATE, AND GIVE THANKS THIS NIGHT. FOR YOUR BROTHER WAS DEAD, AND IS ALIVE AGAIN; WAS LOST, BUT NOW IS FOUND."

UNLESS YOU CHANGE YOUR WAYS, AND BECOME CHILDREN, YOU WILL NOT ENTER THE KINGDOM OF HEAVEN. THE SON OF MAN IS SENT INTO THE WORLD TO SAVE THOSE THAT ARE LOST: FOR IT IS NOT THE WILL OF YOUR FATHER WHO IS IN HEAVEN, THAT EVEN THE LEAST AMONG YOU SHOULD REMAIN OUTSIDE OF THE KINGDOM.

FOR GOD SO LOVED THE WORLD THAT HE SACRIFICED HIS ONLY SON. WHOEVER BELIEVES IN HIM SHALL NOT DIE, BUT RECEIVE EVERLASTING LIFE. DO YOU BELIEVE THIS?
"WHOEVER BELIEVES
IN ME, THOUGH   THEY DIE ON THIS EARTH,
WILL LIVE
             AGAIN."

DISCIPLES AND SER-VANTS

YOU CANNOT ALLOW TWO MASTERS TO

RULE YOUR LIFE. EITHER YOU WILL DISREGARD ONE AND LOVE THE OTHER; OR ELSE CLING TO ONE AND DESPISE THE OTHER. YOU CANNOT SERVE GOD AND REMAIN ENSLAVED TO THE GODS OF THIS WORLD.

WHICH ONE OF YOU, PLANNING TO BUILD A TOWER, WOULD NOT FIRST CAREFULLY ESTIMATE THE COST, MAKING SURE THERE WAS ENOUGH MONEY TO COMPLETE THE CONSTRUCTION? OTHERWISE, HAVING LAID THE FOUNDATION, YOU MAY BE FORCED TO ABANDON THE WORK. THOSE LOOKING ON WOULD LAUGH AND SAY: "YOU BEGAN TO BUILD, BUT NOW YOU ARE RUINED."

A KING WHO PLANS TO WAGE WAR MUST FIRST CONSULT HIS MILITARY ADVISORS TO DETERMINE WHETHER HIS ARMY OF TEN THOUSAND IS CAPABLE OF DEFEATING THE ENEMY'S FORCE OF THIRTY THOUSAND. IF HIS ADVISORS CAN FIND NO HOPE OF VICTORY, HE MUST SEND FORTH HIS AMBASSADORS TO MEET THE ENEMY AND NEGOTIATE PEACE BEFORE THE BATTLE BEGINS.

CONSIDER THAT WHICH YOU POSSESS IN THIS LIFE: FAMILY, MONEY, AND EARTHLY POSSESSIONS. UNLESS YOU ARE WILLING TO MAKE A TOTAL COMMITMENT, EVEN OF WHAT YOU CHERISH, YOU CANNOT TRULY FOLLOW ME.

THE PERSON WHO IS DILIGENT IN SMALL THINGS WILL ALSO BE TRUSTED WITH MUCH; AND THE PERSON WHO IS DISHONEST WITH LITTLE WILL ALSO BE DISHONEST WITH A GREAT DEAL. IF YOU CANNOT BE TRUSTED WITH EARTHLY RICHES, HOW SHALL YOU BE TRUSTED WITH SPIRITUAL TREASURES? AND IF YOU HAVE NOT BEEN FAITHFUL WITH WHAT BELONGS TO OTHERS, HOW SHALL YOU BE TRUSTED WITH RICHES OF YOUR OWN?

I AM SENDING YOU OUT AS SHEEP AMONG WOLVES. BE AS WISE AS SERPENTS, BUT AS HARMLESS AS DOVES.

YOU HAVE SEEN HOW THE EARTHLY RULERS EXERCISE THEIR AUTHORITY, INCONSIDERATE OF THE POOR. THIS IS NOT HOW IT IS TO THOSE IN THE KINGDOM OF GOD. WHOEVER WOULD BE GREAT AMONG YOU MUST FIRST BECOME YOUR SERVANT. AND WHOEVER OF YOU WOULD BE THE GREATEST, MUST FIRST BE SERVANT OF ALL. EVEN SO, I HAVE COME, NOT TO BE SERVED, BUT TO SERVE, AND TO GIVE MY LIFE AS A RANSOM FOR MANY.

IF YOU KNOW THESE THINGS, HAPPY ARE YOU WHEN YOU DO THEM. CONTINUE IN THE LIGHT OF MY WORD. ONLY THEN ARE YOU TRULY MY DISCIPLES.

DO NOT IMITATE THE FALSELY PIOUS, INVENTING LAWS AND

ORDINANCES. THEY VENERATE THEIR RULES AND FAIL TO FULLY OBSERVE EVEN ONE OF THEM. THEY HEAP BURDENS ON THE NECKS OF THEIR FOLLOWERS WITHOUT ATTEMPTING TO LIVE BY THE SAME RULES. THEY GO TO GREAT LENGTHS TO BE SEEN, DRESSING IN EXTRAVAGANT CLOTHING AND BEHAVING WITH GREAT CEREMONY. THEY LOVE TO SIT AT THE HEAD TABLES OR ON THE FRONT ROW, AND TO BE CALLED ESTEEMED OR LEARNED TEACHER. REFUSE TO BE CALLED ESTEEMED OR MASTER; FOR YOU HAVE ONLY ONE MASTER, AND YOU ARE ALL HIS BROTHERS AND SISTERS.

REFRAIN FROM CALLING MEN YOUR SPIRITUAL FATHER; FOR YOU HAVE ONLY ONE FATHER WHO DWELLS IN HEAVEN. NEITHER ALLOW ANYONE TO CALL YOU LEARNED TEACHER; FOR THERE IS ONLY ONE TRUE TEACHER, CHRIST. THE PERSON WHO WOULD BE GREATEST AMONG YOU MUST FIRST BECOME YOUR SERVANT; AND ALL WHO HUMBLE THEMSELVES SHALL BE EXALTED.

WHEN THE MESSIAH RETURNS IN HIS GLORY AND ALL THE HOLY ANGELS ARE WITH HIM, HE WILL SIT UPON THE THRONE OF HIS HEAVENLY GLORY. BEFORE HIM WILL BE GATHERED ALL NATIONS AND HE WILL SEPARATE THEM, AS A SHEPHERD DIVIDES THE SHEEP FROM THE GOATS. THE SHEEP HE WILL SET ON HIS RIGHT HAND, AND THE GOATS ON HIS LEFT.

THEN THE KING OF HEAVEN WILL SAY TO THOSE ON HIS RIGHT: "COME, BLESSED BY MY FATHER; ENTER INTO THE INHERITANCE OF THE KINGDOM, PREPARED FOR YOU SINCE THE FOUNDATION OF THE WORLD. FOR I WAS HUNGRY, AND YOU OFFERED ME FOOD. I WAS THIRSTY, AND YOU BROUGHT ME COLD WATER TO DRINK. I WAS WITHOUT HOME, AND YOU INVITED ME IN. I WAS WITHOUT CLOTHES, AND YOU CLOTHED ME. I WAS ILL, AND YOU CARED FOR ME. I WAS IN PRISON, AND YOU VISITED ME."

THEN THE RIGHTEOUS WILL ANSWER IN AMAZEMENT: "LORD, WHEN DID WE SEE YOU HUNGRY AND FEED YOU; OR THIRSTY AND GIVE YOU DRINK? WHEN DID WE SHELTER OR CLOTHE YOU? DID WE EVER CARE FOR YOU WHEN YOU WERE ILL, OR VISIT YOU IN PRISON?"THE KING WILL REPLY: "TRULY, INASMUCH AS YOU HAVE DONE SUCH THINGS FOR THE LEAST OF MY BROTHERS AND SISTERS, YOU HAVE DONE THE SAME FOR ME."

TO THE ONES ON HIS LEFT, THE KING WILL SAY: "DEPART FROM ME! FOR I WAS HUNGRY, AND YOU GAVE ME NO FOOD. I WAS THIRSTY, AND YOU OFFERED ME NOTHING TO DRINK. I WAS WITHOUT HOME, AND YOU TURNED ME AWAY. I WAS NAKED, AND YOU GAVE ME NO CLOTHES. I WAS SICK, YET YOU DIDN'T CARE FOR ME. I WAS IN PRISON, BUT YOU DIDN'T VISIT ME."

THESE WILL PROTEST: "LORD, WHEN DID WE SEE YOU HUNGRY, OR THIRSTY, OR HOMELESS, OR NAKED, OR SICK, OR IN PRISON, AND FAIL TO COMFORT YOU?"

THE KING WILL ANSWER: "TRULY I SAY TO YOU, INASMUCH AS YOU HAVE FAILED TO DO THESE THINGS FOR THE LEAST OF MY BROTHERS AND SISTERS, YOU HAVE FAILED TO DO THEM FOR ME."

THOSE ON THE LEFT WILL BE SENT AWAY INTO ETERNAL DARKNESS, BUT THE RIGHTEOUS WILL BE USHERED INTO THE KINGDOM OF LIFE.

YOU CALL ME MASTER AND TEACHER. IF I, THEN, AM WILLING TO BE YOUR MOST HUMBLE SERVANT, SHOULD NOT YOU BE WILLING TO SERVE ONE ANOTHER AS WELL? I HAVE LIVED MY LIFE AS AN EXAMPLE BEFORE YOU. IMITATE ME, AND DO THE SAME TO OTHERS AS I HAVE DONE FOR YOU.

"WHOEVER OF YOU WOULD BE THE GREATEST, MUST FIRST BE SERVANT OF ALL."

THE GREAT COMMIS- SION

LET THOSE WHO ARE SPIRITUALLY DEAD
ATTEND TO

THEIR EARTHLY CONCERNS; BUT YOU GO AND PROCLAIM THE COMING OF THE KINGDOM OF GOD TO THE WAITING WORLD.

THERE IS A GREAT HARVEST BEFORE YOU, BUT SADLY, THE LABORERS ARE FEW. PRAY TO THE LORD OF THE HARVEST THAT HE WILL SEND MORE LABORERS TO GATHER IN HIS HARVEST. NO ONE WHO PUTS HIS HAND TO THE PLOUGH AND THEN LOOKS BACK IS SUITABLE FOR THE KINGDOM OF GOD.

IF YOU BELIEVE IN ME, YOU WILL DO THE SAME WORKS THAT I DO. EVEN GREATER WORKS WILL YOU ACCOMPLISH, FOR I MUST RETURN TO MY FATHER IN HEAVEN. IF YOU WISH TO SERVE ME, FOLLOW ME; AND WHERE I AM, THERE YOU, MY SERVANT, WILL BE AS WELL, HONORED BY MY FATHER.

GO ANNOUNCE TO THE WORLD: "THE KINGDOM OF HEAVEN HAS COME TO DWELL AMONG YOU."

HEAL THE SICK, RESTORE THE LEPERS TO HEALTH, RAISE THE DEAD, AND CAST OUT DEVILS! REMEMBER WHAT I HAVE TOLD YOU: "FREELY YOU HAVE RECEIVED. FREELY GIVE!"

IF YOU ARE NOT FOR ME, YOU ARE AGAINST ME; AND THEY THAT DO NOT GATHER WITH ME, SCATTER.

WHENEVER YOU ARE INVITED INTO A HOUSE, OFFER FIRST A BLESSING, AND SAY: "PEACE BE TO THIS HOUSE." IF THOSE IN THE HOUSE ARE FOR PEACE, YOUR BLESSING WILL BE ACCEPTED, AND THEY WILL BE BENEFITED. IF NOT, THE BENEFITS OF YOUR BLESSING WILL RETURN TO YOU.

DO NOT HESITATE TO ACCEPT HOSPITALITY, YET REMAIN PURPOSEFUL. RESIST AIMLESS WANDERING. ENJOY WHATEVER FOOD AND DRINK IS OFFERED YOU, FOR THE PERSON WHO LABORS IS WORTHY OF JUST WAGES.

THOSE WHO ACCEPT YOU ACCEPT ME ALSO, AND THEY THAT ACCEPT ME WELCOME ALSO THE FATHER WHO HAS SENT ME.

BE WARNED: THERE WILL BE THOSE WHO WILL ATTEMPT TO SILENCE YOUR WITNESS OF ME. YOU WILL BE SUMMONED TO COURT AND DEALT WITH UNFAIRLY, AND IMPRISONED ON BEHALF OF ME. BECAUSE OF MY WORDS, YOU WILL BE ASKED TO TESTIFY BEFORE THOSE WHO DO NOT BELIEVE, BEFORE RULERS, GOVERNORS, AND KINGS.

IF YOU ARE ACCUSED AND BROUGHT TO COURT, DO NOT FEAR

AT YOUR LACK OF WORDS. THEY WILL BE GIVEN TO YOU IN THAT INSTANT. YOU NEED NOT RELY ON YOUR WORDS ALONE, FOR THE BREATH OF GOD WILL SPEAK THROUGH YOU. REMEMBER THAT IN THE EARTHLY KINGDOM, NO SERVANT IS GREATER THAN HIS MASTER. IF THEY HAVE PERSECUTED ME, THEY WILL ALSO PERSECUTE YOU, PUNISHING YOU FOR MY CAUSE, NOT REALIZING WHO IT WAS THAT SENT ME INTO THE WORLD. IF, HOWEVER, THEY ACCEPT AND FOLLOW MY MESSAGE, THEY WILL ACCEPT AND FOLLOW YOURS AS WELL.

IF I HAD NOT COME WITH THE MESSAGE OF TRUTH, THE INHABITANTS OF THE WORLD WOULD NOT HAVE BEEN AWARE OF THEIR FAILINGS AND WRONG BEHAVIOR. NO LONGER CAN THEY HIDE BEHIND THEIR FORMER IGNORANCE OF THE TRUTH. IF I HAD NOT PERFORMED MIRACLES AMONG THEM, THEY WOULD NOT HAVE KNOWN THAT THE KINGDOM HAD COME TO DWELL AMONG THEM. NOW, THOSE WHO HAVE REJECTED THE TRUTH HAVE ALSO BEEN WITNESS TO THE MIRACLES, AND

HATE BOTH ME AND MY FATHER. THIS IS COME TO

PASS, THAT THE PROPHECY MIGHT BE FULFILLED: "THEY HAVE HATED ME WITHOUT CAUSE."

TRULY, IT IS A FIRE THAT I HAVE COME TO BRING UPON THE EARTH. HOW I LONG TO SEE IT ABLAZE! DID YOU IMAGINE THAT I HAD COME TO BRING PEACE AND TRANQUILITY? NO, I TELL YOU, I HAVE COME TO SPREAD DIVISION! FROM NOW ON, THERE WILL BE FIVE IN ONE HOUSE, DIVIDED AS TO WHAT THEY SHOULD BELIEVE, THREE AGAINST TWO, AND TWO AGAINST THREE. WHEN YOU ARE CONFRONTED BY THE WORLD'S HATRED, REMEMBER HOW IT HATED ME BEFORE YOUR TIME. AND WHEN THEY PERSECUTE YOU IN ONE PLACE, MOVE ON TO THE NEXT. YOU WILL NOT HAVE REACHED ALL THE PEOPLES OF THE WORLD BEFORE THE MESSIAH RETURNS. IF A CITY REFUSES TO ACCEPT YOU OR HEED YOUR MESSAGE, SHAKE THE DUST OF THAT CITY FROM YOUR FEET AS YOU DEPART. IN THE FINAL DAY OF JUDGMENT, IT WILL HAVE BEEN BETTER TO BE FROM THE LAND OF SODOM AND GOMORRAH THAN FROM SUCH A PLACE.

WHOEVER HEARS THE WORDS THAT YOU SPEAK HEARS ME; AND THOSE THAT DESPISE YOU, BECAUSE OF YOUR WORDS,

DESPISE ME. IN REJECTING ME, THEY REJECT THE FATHER WHO SENT ME. SO, ENDURE THE CRITICISM OF SKEPTICS AND NONBELIEVERS FOR MY SAKE. STAND FIRM, AND IN SO DOING, YOU WILL BE BLESSED.

THESE WORDS I HAVE SPOKEN TO YOU, THAT IN ME, AND IN YOUR OBEDIENCE TO THEM, YOU MIGHT FIND PEACE. IN THE WORLD YOU WILL EXPERIENCE PAIN AND TROUBLE, BUT REJOICE, FOR I HAVE OVERCOME THE WORLD.

CHRIST'S PRAYER FOR HIS DISCIPLES

FATHER, THE HOUR IS COME.

GLORIFY YOUR SON, THAT HE CAN BRING GLORY TO YOU IN RETURN. YOU HAVE GIVEN HIM AUTHORITY OVER EVERY MAN AND WOMAN ON EARTH, THAT HE MIGHT IMPART ETERNAL LIFE TO THOSE YOU HAVE GIVEN HIM.

THIS IS LIFE ETERNAL: THAT ALL MIGHT KNOW THE ONLY TRUE GOD AND JESUS CHRIST, WHOM YOU HAVE SENT. I HAVE GLORIFIED YOU ON EARTH BY COMPLETING THE WORK THAT YOU ENTRUSTED TO ME. NOW, FATHER, REVEAL MY GLORY AS I STAND IN YOUR PRESENCE, THE GLORY I HAVE KNOWN WITH YOU SINCE BEFORE THE WORLD BEGAN. I HAVE REVEALED YOU TO THOSE THAT YOU GAVE ME OUT OF THE WORLD. THEY WERE YOURS, AND YOU GAVE THEM TO ME, AND THEY HAVE ACCEPTED YOUR ETERNAL WORDS. NOW THEY TOO KNOW THAT EVERYTHING YOU HAVE GIVEN ME COMES FROM YOU. I HAVE FAITHFULLY DELIVERED TO THEM THE WORDS THAT YOU GAVE ME; THEY HAVE BELIEVED THEM, AND KNOW IN THEIR HEARTS THAT I HAVE COME FROM GOD, SENT BY YOU ON THEIR BEHALF.

I AM NOT PRAYING FOR THE WORLD, BUT FOR THOSE YOU HAVE GIVEN ME; FOR THEY TRULY ARE YOURS. ALL WHO HAVE BELIEVED IN ME ARE YOURS; AND THEY DO HONOR ME. I AM

RETURNING TO YOU IN HEAVEN; BUT THOSE THAT BELIEVE IN ME REMAIN BEHIND. FATHER, KEEP THEM BY THE POWER OF YOUR NAME; THAT THEY ALL MAY BE ONE, AS WE ARE ONE.

WHILE I WAS WITH THEM IN THE WORLD, I KEPT THEM BY THE POWER THAT YOU GAVE ME, WATCHING OVER THEM, SO THAT NOT ONE WAS LOST, EXCEPT FOR THE SON OF PERDITION, THAT THE SCRIPTURES MIGHT BE FULFILLED. SOON I WILL BE RETURNING TO YOU; SO I AM REQUESTING THESE THINGS WHILE I AM STILL IN THE WORLD, THAT THEY MIGHT EXPERIENCE AND RECEIVE THE FULL REVELATION OF WHAT IS THEIRS.

I HAVE GIVEN THEM YOUR WORD, AND THE WORLD HAS HATED THEM, BECAUSE THEY ARE NO LONGER CHILDREN OF THIS DARK AND DYING PLACE, EVEN AS I AM NOT. I DO NOT ASK THAT YOU REMOVE THEM OUT OF THIS WORLD, BUT THAT YOU KEEP THEM SAFE FROM THE EVIL ONE; FOR THEY ARE NO MORE THE CHILDREN OF DARKNESS THAN I AM. MAKE THEM HOLY BY YOUR TRUTH, FOR YOUR WORD IS TRUTH.

AS YOU HAVE SENT ME INTO THE WORLD, SO I SEND THEM. AND FOR THEIR SAKES I CONSECRATE MYSELF, THAT THEY MAY BE MADE HOLY, AND GROW IN TRUTH. I DO NOT PRAY

FOR THESE ALONE, BUT ALSO FOR THOSE WHO WILL COME TO BELIEVE IN ME BECAUSE OF THE TESTIMONY THAT THEY GIVE. LET THEM ALL BE OF ONE HEART AND MIND, JUST AS YOU AND I ARE ONE: THAT AS YOU ARE IN ME, AND I IN YOU, THEY WILL BE TOGETHER IN US, AND THE WORLD WILL KNOW THAT YOU HAVE SENT ME.

I HAVE GIVEN THEM THE GLORY THAT YOU GAVE ME THAT THEY MAY BE ONE, EVEN AS WE ARE ONE: I IN THEM, AND YOU IN ME, BEING PERFECTED INTO ONE. BECAUSE OF THIS, THE WORLD WILL FULLY UNDERSTAND THAT YOU HAVE SENT ME, AND HAVE LOVED THEM AS MUCH AS YOU HAVE LOVED ME. MAY THEY ONE DAY BE WITH ME WHERE I AM, BEHOLDING MY GLORY, WHICH YOU HAVE LOVINGLY GIVEN ME SINCE THE FOUNDATION OF THE WORLD.

FATHER OF GOODNESS AND TRUTH, THE WORLD HAS NOT KNOWN YOU; BUT I HAVE KNOWN YOU, AND THOSE WHO BELIEVE IN ME KNOW THAT IT IS YOU WHO SENT ME. I HAVE REVEALED YOU TO THEM, AND WILL CONTINUE TO REVEAL YOU TO THEM, SO THAT I, AND THE LOVE YOU HAVE GIVEN ME, MAY FULLY DWELL IN THEIR HEARTS.

THE PROMISE

THIS GENERA- TION

WHOEVER IS ASHAMED OF
ME AND

OF MY WORDS IN THESE DAYS OF SIN AND NON-BELIEF, OF THAT PERSON, THE SON OF MAN WILL BE ASHAMED WHEN HE RETURNS IN THE GLORY OF HIS FATHER WITH THE HOLY ANGELS.

STILL NON-BELIEVING, THIS OBSTINATE GENERATION CLAMOURS FOR A SIGN; BUT NO SIGN WILL BE GRANTED OTHER THAN THE SIGN THAT WAS GIVEN TO THE PROPHET JONAH. FOR JUST AS JONAH WAS IN THE GREAT DEEP FOR THREE DAYS AND NIGHTS, SO THE SON OF MAN WILL BE THREE DAYS AND NIGHTS ENTOMBED IN THE EARTH.

THERE WILL COME A DAY WHEN THE INHABITANTS OF NINEVEH, CALLED THE CITY OF THIEVES, WILL STAND AND PASS JUDGMENT ON THIS GENERATION AND CONDEMN IT. FOR THEY REPENTED BECAUSE OF THE PREACHING OF JONAH, AND NOW ONE GREATER THAN JONAH STANDS BEFORE YOU.

THE QUEEN OF SHEBA WILL ALSO RISE TO PASS JUDGMENT ON THIS GENERATION AND CONDEMN IT; FOR SHE TRAVELED A GREAT DISTANCE TO

HEAR THE WISDOM OF SOLOMON, AND BEHOLD, ONE GREATER THAN SOLOMON HAS COME.

HOW CAN I DESCRIBE THIS GENERATION? THEY ARE LIKE CHILDREN SITTING IN THE MARKET PLACE, CALLING TO THEIR FRIENDS: "WE HAVE PLAYED MERRILY ON OUR FLUTES; BUT YOU WOULD NOT DANCE OR SING. WE HAVE PLAYED A DIRGE; BUT YOU HAVE REFUSED TO BE SAD."

JOHN, THE FORERUNNER, CAME AND LIVED AMONG YOU IN GREAT AUSTERITY. EVERYONE SAID: "HE MUST BE POSSESSED OF A DEMON."

NOW THE SON OF MAN HAS COME TO YOU, ENJOYING LIFE, AND YOU SAY: "HE IS A DRUNKARD AND A GLUTTON, AND THE FRIEND OF SINNERS!" WITH SUCH BRILLIANCE, YOU JUSTIFY YOUR OWN INCONSISTENCY.

OH GENERATION, WHO LIVE YOUR LIVES BASED ON LIES: HOW CAN YOU, BEING WITHOUT TRUTH, SAY ANYTHING WORTH HEARING? FOR OUT OF THE ABUNDANCE OF THE HEART, THE MOUTH SPEAKS.

WHEN IT IS EVENING, YOU SAY: "IT WILL BE FAIR WEATHER, FOR THE SKY IS RED."

IN THE MORNING YOU SAY: "IT WILL BE FOUL WEATHER TODAY, FOR THE SKY IS THREATENING."

WITH ACCURACY YOU FORECAST A CHANGE IN THE WEATHER. HOW IS IT THAT YOU HAVE FAILED TO DISCERN THE SIGNS OF THE TIMES?

COME UNTO ME ALL WHO ARE TIRED, OPPRESSED, AND SICK OF LIFE, AND I WILL GIVE YOU WONDERFUL REST! RECEIVE MY WORDS AND LET ME TEACH YOU, FOR I AM GENTLE AND KIND. YOU WILL FIND REST FOR YOUR SOULS. THAT WHICH I ASK OF YOU IS FOR YOUR BENEFIT, AND THAT WHICH I DEMAND OF YOU IS LIGHT.

THOSE WHO HAVE CHOSEN TO FOLLOW ME IN THIS GENERATION WILL ONE DAY SIT UPON THRONES AND JUDGE KINGDOMS AND KINGS WHO HAVE HARDENED THEIR HEARTS AND TURNED AWAY FROM THESE RIGHTEOUS WORDS.

A PLACE FOR YOU

I GO TO PREPARE A PLACE FOR YOU.

KNOW THIS: IF I GO AND
YOU, I WILL COME AGAIN,
THERE WITH ME; SO THAT
MAY BE ALSO. LET NOT YO
YOU BELIEVE IN GOD; BELI
FATHER'S HOUSE ARE MAN\
NOT SO, I WOULD HAVE TOL
BUT I WILL COME AGAIN TO YOU. IF YOU TRULY
LOVED ME YOU WOULD REJOICE, BECAUSE I RETURN
TO THE FATHER.

DO NOT MARVEL WHEN I SAY: FOR A LITTLE WHILE,
YOU WILL NOT SEE ME; BUT NOT LONG AFTER THAT,
YOU WILL SEE ME AGAIN. YOU WILL WEEP AND BE
SAD, BUT THE WORLD WILL REJOICE. YOU WILL BE
SORROWFUL, BUT YOUR SORROW WILL BE TURNED
TO JOY.

A WOMAN, WHEN SHE IS IN CHILDBIRTH, KNOWS
PAIN AND AGONY; BUT AS SOON AS THE CHILD IS
DELIVERED SHE FORGETS HER SUFFERING, REJOICING
THAT HER CHILD IS BORN INTO THE WORLD. FOR A
MOMENT YOU MAY EXPERIENCE SORROW; BUT I WILL
SEE YOU AGAIN, AND YOUR HEART WILL REJOICE,
AND NO ONE WILL BE ABLE TO TAKE YOUR JOY
FROM YOU.

PROMISE OF THE SPIRIT

IT IS THE SPIRIT THAT

HAS THE POWER TO GIVE LIFE.

IF YOU LOVE ME, THEN KEEP MY COMMANDMENTS. AND I WILL PRAY TO THE FATHER, AND HE WILL GIVE YOU ANOTHER COMFORTER TO BE WITH YOU FOREVER. HIS IS THE BREATH OF TRUTH. THE WORLD DOES NOT ACCEPT HIM, BECAUSE IT NEITHER SEES HIM NOR KNOWS HIM. BUT YOU WILL KNOW HIM, FOR HE WILL DWELL WITH YOU, AND IN YOU.

I WILL NOT LEAVE YOU COMFORTLESS. NOW IT IS NECESSARY FOR YOU THAT I GO AWAY; FOR IF I DO NOT LEAVE, THE COMFORTER, THE VERY BREATH OF GOD, WILL NOT COME TO DWELL AMONG YOU. IF I DEPART, I WILL SEND HIM TO YOU.

WHEN HE HAS COME, HE WILL REVEAL TO THE WORLD WHAT IS SIN, AND WHAT IS RIGHTEOUSNESS AND JUDGMENT. SIN, BECAUSE YOU DO NOT BELIEVE IN ME; RIGHTEOUSNESS, BECAUSE I GO TO MY FATHER, AND YOU WILL NOT SEE ME; JUDGMENT, BECAUSE THE OPPRESSIVE POWER OF THE PRINCE OF THIS WORLD HAS BEEN BROKEN.

I HAVE MANY MORE THINGS TO SAY TO YOU, BUT YOU CANNOT UNDERSTAND THEM JUST NOW. HOWEVER, WHEN THE BREATH OF GOD HAS COME, HE WILL GUIDE YOU INTO ALL TRUTH, FOR HE WILL NOT SPEAK OF HIMSELF; BUT WHATEVER HE HEARS, THAT HE WILL SPEAK, SHOWING YOU THOSE THINGS THAT ARE TO COME.

HE WILL PRAISE ME AND GLORIFY ME, BY REVEALING MY GLORY TO YOU. ALL OF THE FATHER'S GLORY IS MINE AS WELL. THIS IS WHY I AM ABLE TO MAKE THIS PROMISE TO YOU: THE SPIRIT WILL REVEAL MY DIVINE NATURE TO YOU. IF YOUR CHILD ASKED OF YOU BREAD, WOULD YOU OFFER A STONE? IF YOUR CHILD ASKED FISH TO EAT, WOULD YOU OFFER A SNAKE? WOULD YOU SERVE A SCORPION TO THE LITTLE ONES WHO ASK FOR AN EGG?

IF YOU THEN, BEING OF THIS EARTH, KNOW HOW TO PROVIDE GOOD THINGS FOR YOUR CHILDREN, HOW MUCH MORE WILL YOUR HEAVENLY FATHER GIVE THE BREATH OF GOD TO THOSE WHO ASK HIM?

WHEN THE COMFORTER, THE SPIRIT OF TRUTH,
WHOM I WILL SEND TO YOU FROM THE FATHER
HAS COME, HE WILL TESTIFY OF ME. HE WILL
TEACH YOU ALL THINGS, AND WILL REMIND YOU
OF ALL THAT I HAVE TOLD YOU.
"WHEN THE BREATH   OF GOD HAS
COME,
HE WILL GUIDE YOU INTO ALL
      TRUTH."

AN INVI-
TATION
TO LIFE

**EVERYONE WHO BELIEVES
IN THE**

SON WILL HAVE LIFE EVERLASTING.

A WEALTHY MAN PLANNED A GREAT BANQUET, AND INVITED MANY GUESTS. WHEN THE PREPARATIONS WERE COMPLETED, HE SENT HIS SERVANT TO GATHER THOSE WHO HAD BEEN INVITED. "COME," HE SAID, "FOR ALL THINGS ARE READY."

BUT ALL THOSE WHO HAD BEEN INVITED BEGAN TO MAKE EXCUSES.

THE FIRST REPLIED: "I HAVE JUST PURCHASED A PIECE OF LAND, AND I MUST GO AND LOOK AT IT AGAIN. PLEASE HAVE ME EXCUSED."

THE SECOND SAID: "I HAVE JUST PURCHASED A HERD OF CATTLE, AND I MUST GO AND EXAMINE IT. PLEASE HAVE ME EXCUSED."

A THIRD ANSWERED: "I HAVE RECENTLY BEEN MARRIED, AND FOR THIS, I CANNOT ATTEND."

FINALLY, THE SERVANT RETURNED AND REPORTED WHAT HAD HAPPENED. HEARING THE DISAPPOINTING

NEWS, THE MASTER COMMANDED: "GO QUICKLY INTO THE STREETS OF THE CITY, AND GATHER THE POOR, THE LAME, THE ILL, AND THE BLIND."

THE SERVANT HURRIED TO DO THIS AND SOON RETURNED, SAYING: "SIR, I HAVE DONE AS YOU COMMANDED, AND STILL THERE IS ROOM AT THE TABLE."

"GO THEN," THE RICH MAN REPLIED, "ALONG THE HIGHWAYS AND AMONG THE FIELDS, AND URGE THOSE YOU MEET TO COME IN, THAT MY TABLE MIGHT BE FILLED. FOR I SAY TO YOU: NONE OF THOSE THAT WERE ORIGINALLY INVITED WILL TASTE OF THE BANQUET THAT I HAD PREPARED FOR THEM."

WHOEVER HEARS MY WORD AND BELIEVES IN THE ONE WHO HAS SENT ME WILL FIND ETERNAL LIFE AND NOT BE CONDEMNED. INSTEAD, THEY WILL PASS FROM DEATH UNTO LIFE. DO NOT BE AMAZED AT THIS, FOR THE

TIME IS COMING WHEN EVEN THE DEAD WILL HEAR THE VOICE OF THE SON OF GOD, AND THOSE WHO HEAR HIS VOICE SHALL LIVE. IN THEIR GRAVES, THE DEAD WILL RECOGNIZE HIS VOICE AND BE RAISED UP; THOSE THAT HAVE DONE GOOD WILL BE RAISED TO NEW LIFE, AND THOSE WHO HAVE LIVED WRONGFULLY WILL BE RAISED TO CONDEMNATION.

HEREIN LIES THE WAY TO ETERNAL LIFE: KNOW THE ONLY TRUE GOD AND JESUS CHRIST, THE ONE SENT TO YOU BY GOD. TAKE MY WORDS TO HEART. FOR GOD SO LOVED THE WORLD THAT HE OFFERED HIS ONLY SON, A LIVING SACRIFICE, THAT WHOEVER BELIEVES IN HIM WILL NOT PERISH, BUT BE REDEEMED AND HAVE EVERLASTING LIFE. THIS GOOD NEWS OF THE KINGDOM SHALL BE PREACHED TO THE ENTIRE WORLD AS A WITNESS TO ALL NATIONS; AND THEN SHALL THE END COME.

THE END TIMES

TRULY I SAY UNTO YOU:

THIS GENERATION SHALL NOT PASS UNTIL ALL OF THESE THINGS ARE FULFILLED.

ONCE THERE WAS A LANDOWNER WHO PLANTED A VINEYARD, AND ON THE GROUNDS HE INSTALLED A WINEPRESS. AROUND THE VINEYARD HE BUILT A TALL FENCE, ERECTING EVEN A TOWER. THEN HE RENTED HIS VINEYARD TO VINE KEEPERS, AND VOYAGED TO A DISTANT COUNTRY.

WHEN THE TIME OF THE HARVEST APPROACHED, THE LANDOWNER SENT HIS SERVANTS TO THE VINE KEEPERS TO COLLECT HIS PROFITS. BUT THE VINE KEEPERS AMBUSHED HIS SERVANTS, BEAT ONE, KILLED ANOTHER, AND DROVE THE THIRD OFF WITH STONES.

AGAIN, THE LANDOWNER SENT SERVANTS TO COLLECT HIS PROFITS. THIS TIME HE SENT A LARGER GROUP THAN THE FIRST, BUT THEY MET WITH A SIMILAR FATE.

FINALLY THE LANDOWNER SENT HIS ONLY SON, REASONING, "AT LEAST THEY WILL RESPECT MY ONLY SON."

WHEN THE VINE KEEPERS SAW THE SON APPROACHING, HOWEVER, THEY PLOTTED FOOLISHLY AMONG THEMSELVES: "HERE BEFORE US IS THE HEIR TO THE VINEYARD. IF WE KILL HIM, HIS INHERITANCE WILL BE OURS."

SO PLOTTING, THEY BOUND THE SON, DRAGGED HIM OUTSIDE THE VINEYARD WALLS, AND TOOK HIS LIFE. I ASK YOU: WHEN, FINALLY, THE LANDOWNER OF THE VINEYARD RETURNS, WHAT WILL BE THE FATE OF THE WICKED VINE KEEPERS?

MY PEOPLE, MY PEOPLE, YOU WHO HAVE KILLED THE PROPHETS, AND SPURNED THOSE SENT TO YOU, HOW OFTEN WOULD I HAVE GATHERED YOU, EVEN AS A HEN SHELTERS HER CHICKS BENEATH HER WINGS, AND YET YOU WOULD NOT! BEHOLD, YOUR HOUSE IS LEFT DESOLATE; AND YOU WILL NOT SEE ME AGAIN UNTIL THE TIME WHEN ALL WILL SAY: "BLESSED IS HE WHO COMES IN THE NAME OF THE LORD."

IF YOU HAD ONLY KNOWN, IN THIS YOUR DAY OF SALVATION, THAT ETERNAL PEACE WAS SO NEAR

AT HAND! BUT NOW IT IS HIDDEN FROM YOUR EYES. THE POWERS OF THE HEAVENS WILL BE SHAKEN, AND PEOPLE'S HEARTS WILL FAIL THEM FOR FEAR, ANTICIPATING THE CALAMITIES THAT ARE DESTINED FOR THIS WORLD.

WHEN THE END TIME COMES, AND YOU SEE THE "ABOMINATION OF DESOLATION" SPOKEN OF BY DANIEL THE PROPHET STANDING IN THE SACRED PLACE, THEN IT IS TIME FOR THOSE THAT DWELL IN THE CITIES TO FLEE TO THE MOUNTAINS. LET NO ONE ON THE HOUSETOPS TURN TO SAVE ANYTHING THAT IS IN THE HOUSE; NEITHER LET THOSE WORKING IN THE FIELD GO BACK TO FETCH THEIR BELONGINGS. SORROW, TO THOSE WHO BEAR CHILDREN IN THOSE DAYS! MAY THEIR FLIGHT NOT BE IN WINTER OR ON THE SABBATH: FOR THERE WILL BE GREAT DISTRESS, UNEQUALLED SINCE TIME BEGAN. UNLESS SUCH DAYS BE SHORTENED, FEW WOULD ENDURE: AND YET THOSE DAYS SHALL INDEED BE SHORTENED, FOR THE SAKE OF GOD'S CHOSEN ONES.

THE DAY WILL COME WHEN YOUR ENEMIES WILL LAY A TRENCH AROUND YOUR WALLS, AND HEM YOU IN ON EVERY SIDE. THEY WILL HURL YOU TO THE DUST AND YOUR CHILDREN WITH YOU, AND WILL NOT LEAVE ONE STONE STANDING UPON ANOTHER, ALL THIS BECAUSE YOU FAILED TO RECOGNIZE THE APPOINTED TIME WHEN GOD HIMSELF MOVED AMONG YOU.

DO YOU SEE STANDING THESE TEMPLE WALLS? TRULY I SAY TO YOU, NOT ONE STONE WILL BE LEFT UPRIGHT! JERUSALEM WILL BE TRAMPLED UNDERFOOT BY THE GENTILES UNTIL THE TIMES OF THE GENTILES BE FULFILLED.

WHEN YOU HEAR OF WARS AND THE TURMOIL OF DESTRUCTION; DO NOT LET YOUR HEARTS FILL WITH FEAR, FOR THESE THINGS MUST FIRST COME TO PASS; THE END IS NOT YET. NATION WILL RISE AGAINST NATION, AND KINGDOM AGAINST KINGDOM. FEARFUL SIGHTS AND GREAT SIGNS WILL APPEAR IN THE HEAVENS. THERE WILL BE SIGNS IN THE SUN, AND IN THE MOON, AND IN THE STARS. ON THE EARTH WILL BE GREAT ADVERSITY BETWEEN

THE NATIONS, AND PERPLEXITY, ROARING LIKE THE SEA'S MIGHTY WAVES. FAMINES, PLAGUES, AND EARTHQUAKES WILL INCREASE. ALL THESE ARE THE BEGINNINGS OF SORROW. BECAUSE EVIL WILL ABOUND, THE LOVE OF MANY WILL TURN COLD.

YOU WILL BE BETRAYED, AND CONDEMNED TO DEATH, AND HATED BY ALL NATIONS FOR MY NAME'S SAKE. REMAIN WATCHFUL, AND PRAY ALWAYS THAT YOU MAY BE COUNTED WORTHY TO ESCAPE THESE THINGS THAT ARE COMING TO PASS, AND TO STAND, JUSTIFIED, BEFORE THE MESSIAH, THE SON OF MAN.

CONSIDER THE FIG TREE, AND LEARN FROM IT. WHEN ITS BRANCHES GROW FULL OF SAP AND PRODUCE NEW LEAVES, ONE KNOWS THAT SUMMER IS DRAWING NEAR. EVEN SO, NO ONE KNOWS THE EXACT DAY, OR THE PRECISE HOUR OF MESSIAH'S RETURNING; NOT EVEN THE ANGELS WHO ARE IN HEAVEN, BUT ONLY MY FATHER. YET SEEING ALL OF THESE EVENTS BEGINNING TO COME TO PASS, KNOW IN YOUR HEART THAT THE DAY OF COMPLETION DRAWS NEAR.

THE RE-
TURN

WATCH THEREFORE,

FOR YOU KNOW NOT THE HOUR WHEN YOUR LORD WILL COME.

BEWARE THAT NO MAN DECEIVE YOU; FOR IN THE END TIMES, MANY WILL COME USING MY NAME, SAYING, "I AM CHRIST," AND WILL DECEIVE MANY. FALSE PROPHETS WILL ARISE; AND THEY TOO WILL LEAD MANY INTO BELIEVING THEIR LIES.

DO NOT BELIEVE THOSE WHO TELL YOU: "I HAVE FOUND ONE LIKE CHRIST." THERE WILL ARISE MANY DECEITFUL IMITATORS AND FALSE PROPHETS EXHIBITING "SIGNS" AND "WONDERS," SO THAT EVEN THE ELECT WILL BE DECEIVED.

SOME AMONG YOU WILL SAY, "BEHOLD, ONE LIKE CHRIST IS IN THE DESERT." DO NOT HURRY OUT LOOKING FOR ME. OR IF THEY SAY, "CHRIST HAS COME, AND IS IN A SECRET LOCATION THAT I ALONE KNOW OF," DO NOT BELIEVE IT. FOR EVEN AS THE LIGHTNING FLASHES ACROSS THE SKY, ILLUMINATING THE HEAVENS FROM THE EAST TO THE WEST, SO WILL BE THE COMING OF THE SON OF MAN.

AT THE END OF TIME, THE SIGN OF THE SON OF MAN WILL APPEAR IN THE HEAVENS, CAUSING THE NATIONS

OF THE EARTH TO TREMBLE. ALL WILL SEE THE MESSIAH, THE SON OF MAN, APPEARING WITH POWER AND GREAT GLORY; AND THEY WILL SEE THE SON OF MAN SITTING ON THE RIGHT HAND OF THE LIVING GOD, RETURNING ON THE CLOUDS OF HEAVEN. AND HE WILL SEND HIS ANGELS WITH THE GREAT SOUND OF A TRUMPET, AND THEY WILL GATHER TOGETHER HIS CHOSEN ONES AS FROM THE FOUR WINDS, FROM THE FARTHEST ENDS OF THE HEAVENS AND EARTH, AND REWARD EVERYONE ACCORDING TO HIS WORKS.

AS IT WAS IN THE DAYS OF NOAH, SO WILL IT BE AT THE TIME OF THE COMING OF THE SON OF MAN. IN THE DAYS THAT PRECEDED THE GREAT FLOOD, THEY WERE EATING AND DRINKING, MARRYING AND GIVING IN MARRIAGE, AND CARELESSLY CELEBRATING, UNTIL THE DAY THAT NOAH ENTERED INTO THE ARK.

IT WAS THE SAME IN THE DAYS OF LOT. MEN AND WOMEN ATE AND DRANK, BOUGHT AND SOLD, PLANTED AND BUILT. BUT ON THE DAY THAT LOT DEPARTED FROM SODOM, IT RAINED FIRE AND MOLTEN SULFUR FROM HEAVEN, AND DESTROYED THEM ALL. SO WILL IT BE ON THE DAY THAT THE SON OF MAN IS REVEALED.

DO NOT LET YOUR HEART BE OVERWHELMED BY THE

PURSUIT OF EARTHLY PLEASURE OR THE ANXIETIES OF LIFE. LET NOT MY RETURNING FIND YOU UNPREPARED; FOR LIKE THE SPRINGING OF A TRAP WILL IT SUDDENLY COME UPON THE EARTH.

TWO WILL BE WORKING IN A FIELD. ONE WILL BE TAKEN AND THE OTHER LEFT BEHIND. TWO WOMEN WILL BE GRINDING AT A MILL. ONE WILL BE TAKEN, AND THE OTHER LEFT BEHIND. WATCH THEREFORE, FOR YOU KNOW NOT IN WHICH HOUR YOUR LORD WILL RETURN. BUT DO KNOW THIS: THAT IF THOSE IN THE HOUSE HAD KNOWN THE HOUR OF THE THIEF'S COMING, THEY WOULD HAVE REMAINED WATCHFUL, AND WOULD NOT HAVE LET THEIR STORES BE PLUNDERED.

OF THIS I ASSURE YOU, PROPHETS AND KINGS HAVE DESIRED TO SEE THE THINGS THAT YOU NOW SEE, AND DID NOT, OR TO HEAR THE THINGS YOU NOW HEAR, AND DID NOT HAVE THE OPPORTUNITY TO HEAR THEM. YOU, INSTEAD, HAVE BOTH SEEN AND HEARD ALL OF THESE PROPHECIES COME TO PASS.

PREPARE YOUR HEART; FOR IN THE HOUR THAT YOU LEAST EXPECT IT, THE SON OF MAN WILL COME.

HEAR THE STORY OF TEN BRIDESMAIDS WHO CARRIED

THEIR LAMPS OUT TO MEET THE BRIDEGROOM TO ILLUMINATE THE PATH OF HIS ARRIVAL. THIS GROUP WAS COMPRISED OF FIVE WISE AND FIVE FOOLISH WOMEN. THOSE THAT WERE FOOLISH REMEMBERED THEIR LAMPS, BUT NOT EXTRA FUEL, WHILE THE WISE CARRIED BOTH THEIR LAMPS AND ADDED FUEL. THE BRIDEGROOM'S COMING WAS DELAYED, AND THEY BEGAN TO GROW TIRED AND FALL ASLEEP.

FINALLY, AT MIDNIGHT, THERE AROSE A CRY: "BEHOLD, THE BRIDEGROOM APPROACHES! THE TIME HAS COME TO GO OUT TO MEET HIM."

HURRIEDLY, THE BRIDESMAIDS BEGAN PREPARING THEIR LAMPS. THEN THE FOOLISH SAID TO THE WISE: "GIVE US SOME OF YOUR FUEL; FOR OUR LAMPS HAVE BURNED OUT IN THE NIGHT."

"WE CANNOT," THE WISE REPLIED, "FOR THERE IS NOT ENOUGH FUEL FOR BOTH YOUR LAMPS AND OURS. GO QUICKLY, WAKE THOSE THAT SELL FUEL, AND BUY EXTRA FOR YOURSELVES."

BUT WHILE THEY WERE OFF SEARCHING FOR FUEL, THE BRIDEGROOM CAME; AND THOSE WHO WERE READY WENT WITH HIM TO THE MARRIAGE CELEBRATION, AND

BEHIND THEM THE DOOR WAS SHUT.

SOME TIME LATER, THE FOOLISH BRIDESMAIDS RETURNED AND BEGAN TO CALL OUT PLAINTIVELY: "LORD, LORD, LET US IN."

BUT HE ANSWERED AND SAID: "TRULY I SAY TO YOU, I DO NOT KNOW WHO YOU ARE."

BLESSED ARE THOSE SERVANTS WHOM THE LORD, WHEN HE COMES, FINDS READY AND ANTICIPATING HIS ARRIVAL, EVEN IF HE SHOULD COME IN THE MIDDLE OF THE NIGHT OR AT DAWNING OF THE DAY. TRULY I SAY, THAT HE WILL ADORN HIMSELF IN HIS BANQUET CLOTHES AND INVITE SUCH SERVANTS TO SIT DOWN WITH HIM AT THE TABLE OF FEASTING, RISING HIMSELF TO SERVE THEM AS HONORED GUESTS!

BE ALWAYS WATCHFUL; FOR YOU DO NOT KNOW THE DAY OR THE HOUR WHEN THE SON OF MAN WILL RETURN. LIVE YOUR LIFE IN A PREPARED MANNER, YOUR LIGHTS BURNING BRIGHTLY, LIKE THOSE SERVANTS WHO WAIT WITH EXPECTANCY FOR THE SOUND OF THE LORD'S APPROACHING.

IT IS EASIER FOR HEAVEN AND EARTH TO PASS AWAY THAN FOR ONE OF THESE WORDS TO FAIL.

THE LAST DAYS OF
CHRIST ON THE

EARTH

THE BETRAY-AL

ALL THINGS THAT WERE

WRITTEN BY THE PROPHETS CONCERNING THE MESSIAH SHALL BE FULFILLED. HE WILL BE DELIVERED INTO THE CUSTODY OF THE HEATHEN, MOCKED, TREATED SPITEFULLY, AND MISUSED. THEY WILL BEAT HIM AND PUT HIM TO DEATH; BUT ON THE THIRD DAY HE WILL RISE AGAIN.

SOON I MUST LEAVE THIS EARTH. FOR A TIME YOU CANNOT JOIN ME IN THE PLACE WHERE I AM GOING, SO LET US CELEBRATE ONE LAST PASSOVER TOGETHER. THE TIME APPROACHES WHEN I MUST SUFFER; FOR I TELL YOU IN TRUTH: I WILL NOT EAT OF THE PASSOVER AGAIN UNTIL ALL THAT IT SIGNIFIES IS FULFILLED IN THE KINGDOM OF GOD; NOR WILL I DRINK OF THE FRUIT OF THE VINE UNTIL THE KINGDOM OF GOD HAS COME.

THIS BREAD OF THE PASSOVER REPRESENTS MY BODY, WHICH IS GIVEN FOR YOU. EAT IT IN REMEMBRANCE OF ME. THE WINE REPRESENTS GOD'S NEW COVENANT OF SALVATION, SEALED BY MY BLOOD, WHICH I DO SHED ON YOUR BEHALF.

I MUST GIVE MY LIFE, AS WAS FORETOLD BY THE PROPHETS. WHAT SORROW AWAITS THE ONE WHO BETRAYS THE SON OF MAN. IT WOULD HAVE BEEN BETTER IF HE HAD NOT BEEN

BORN. I AM NOT SAYING THIS OF YOU, FOR I KNOW VERY WELL THOSE WHOM I HAVE CHOSEN; BUT IT HAS BEEN WRITTEN: "ONE WHO SHARES MY BREAD WILL BETRAY ME." I TELL YOU THIS BEFORE IT COMES TO PASS, SO THAT AFTERWARDS YOU WILL BELIEVE IN ME.

YOU BOAST THAT YOU ARE WILLING TO LAY DOWN YOUR LIFE FOR MY SAKE! SADLY, YOU WILL ALL DESERT ME ON THE NIGHT OF MY BETRAYAL, AS THE PROPHETS HAVE WRITTEN: "I WILL STRIKE THE SHEPHERD, AND THE SHEEP WILL BE SCATTERED."

OH! FATHER! HEAR MY PRAYER! IF IT IS POSSIBLE, LET THIS ORDEAL PASS FROM ME! NEVERTHELESS NOT MY WILL, BUT YOUR WILL BE FINISHED.

BEHOLD, THE HOUR HAS COME FOR THE SON OF MAN TO BE ABANDONED INTO THE HANDS OF EVILDOERS. BEWARE! THOSE WHO LIVE BY THE SWORD WILL DIE BY THE SWORD.

HOW CAN IT BE THAT YOU BETRAY THE SON OF MAN WITH A KISS, ARRESTING ME LIKE A COMMON THIEF, CARRYING SWORDS AND CLUBS? DAILY I WAS AMONG YOU IN THE

TEMPLE, AND YOU NEVER LAID A HAND ON ME. BUT THIS IS YOUR HOUR, AND THE POWER OF DARKNESS IS AT WORK.

DO YOU NOT REALIZE THAT I COULD PRAY TO MY FATHER, AND HE COULD SEND DOWN TWELVE LEGIONS OF ANGELS FOR MY DEFENSE? HOW THEN COULD THE SCRIPTURES BE FULFILLED THAT PREDICT IT MUST HAPPEN THIS WAY? NOW THE SON OF MAN WILL BE GLORIFIED, AND GOD WILL BE MAGNIFIED IN HIM.

THE TRI-AL AND THE CROSS

YOU HAVE NO POWER AT ALL AGAINST

ME UNLESS IT IS GIVEN TO YOU FROM ABOVE.

WHY DO YOU PROSECUTE ME BY THESE ACCUSATIONS? INTERROGATE THOSE WHO HEARD ME TEACH. THEY KNOW VERY WELL THE THINGS I HAVE SAID. I DID NOT SPREAD MY MESSAGE IN SECRET, BUT SPOKE OPENLY FOR THE WORLD TO HEAR, TEACHING PUBLICLY IN PLACES OF WORSHIP AND THE COURTYARDS OF THE TEMPLE WHERE MY FOLLOWERS GATHERED.

IF WHAT I HAVE SAID VIOLATES YOUR LAWS, THEN GIVE EVIDENCE OF THIS. BUT IF I HAVE SPOKEN THE TRUTH, THEN WHY DO YOU STRIKE ME?

MY KINGDOM IS NOT OF THIS WORLD. IF MY KINGDOM WERE OF THIS WORLD, MY FOLLOWERS WOULD HAVE TAKEN UP ARMS TO DEFEND IT, THAT I SHOULD NOT BE DELIVERED INTO YOUR HANDS. BUT MINE IS NOT AN EARTHLY KINGDOM. YET YOU ARE RIGHT WHEN YOU ACCUSE ME OF BEING A KING. TO THIS END WAS I BORN, AND FOR THIS PURPOSE I CAME INTO THE WORLD: THAT I SHOULD BE A WITNESS TO THE TRUTH. ALL WHO LOVE THE TRUTH RECOGNIZE MY MESSAGE. NOW WILL

THE PRINCE OF THIS WORLD BE OVERTHROWN, AND IF I BE LIFTED UP FROM THE EARTH, I WILL DRAW ALL PEOPLE TO ME.

THIS ABOVE ALL IS WHY MY FATHER LOVES ME; FOR I LAY DOWN MY LIFE WILLINGLY THAT I MIGHT TAKE IT UP AGAIN. NO MAN TAKES IT FROM ME, BUT I LAY IT DOWN OF MY OWN FREE WILL. I HAVE THE POWER TO LAY IT DOWN; AND I HAVE THE POWER TO TAKE IT UP AGAIN. THE FATHER HAS GIVEN ME THIS POWER.

FATHER, FORGIVE THEM, FOR THEY KNOW NOT WHAT THEY DO.

MY GOD, MY GOD, WHY HAVE YOU FORSAKEN ME?

"I LAY DOWN MY LIFE   WILLINGLY   THAT I MIGHT TAKE IT UP
                AGAIN."

FOLLOW-ING THE RESUR-RECTION

OH FOOLS,

SO SLOW TO BELIEVE ALL THAT THE PROPHETS HAVE SPOKEN! SHOULD NOT CHRIST HAVE SUFFERED ALL OF THESE THINGS AND THEN ENTER INTO HIS GLORY? BE FAITHLESS NO LONGER, BUT BELIEVE.

THIS IS WHAT I HAVE TOLD YOU FROM THE BEGINNING, THAT ALL THINGS MUST BE FULFILLED WHICH ARE WRITTEN IN THE LAW OF MOSES, AND BY THE PROPHETS, AND BY THE PSALM-WRITERS, CONCERNING ME! CHRIST MUST SUFFER, AND THEN RISE FROM THE DEAD ON THE THIRD DAY; THAT REPENTANCE AND FORGIVENESS OF SINS MIGHT BE PREACHED IN HIS NAME AMONG ALL NATIONS, BEGINNING IN JERUSALEM.

I KNOW FROM WHERE I HAVE COME, AND WHERE I WILL GO. YOU CANNOT TELL FROM WHERE I HAVE COME, OR WHERE I AM GOING. YOU ARE FROM THE EARTH. I AM FROM ABOVE. YOU ARE OF THIS WORLD. I AM NOT OF THIS WORLD.

NO ONE HAS ASCENDED UP TO HEAVEN, EXCEPT HE THAT
HAS COME DOWN FROM HEAVEN, THE SON OF GOD WHO

IS IN HEAVEN. GO, TELL MY BROTHERS THAT I WILL ASCEND TO MY FATHER, AND YOUR FATHER; AND TO MY GOD, AND YOUR GOD.

WHY ARE YOU TROUBLED, ALLOWING DOUBT TO FILL YOUR MINDS? BE IN PEACE. WITNESS MY HANDS AND MY FEET. TOUCH ME, AND VERIFY MY RESURRECTED BODY; FOR A GHOST DOES NOT APPEAR HAVING FLESH AND BONES. BECAUSE YOU HAVE SEEN ME, YOU BELIEVE. MORE BLESSED ARE THOSE WHO COME AFTER YOU, WHO HAVING NOT SEEN ME, BELIEVE.

IN A LITTLE WHILE, THE WORLD WILL SEE ME NO MORE; BUT MY PRESENCE WILL REMAIN WITH YOU; AND BECAUSE I LIVE, YOU WILL LIVE ALSO.

"MORE BLESSED
ARE THOSE   WHO COME AFTER YOU,
WHO HAVING NOT SEEN ME,
BELIEVE."

AL-
WAYS

AS MY FATHER HAS SENT ME, SO I SEND YOU.

GO THEREFORE, AND TEACH ALL NATIONS, BAPTIZING THEM IN THE NAME OF THE FATHER AND THE SON AND THE HOLY SPIRIT. GO INTO THE WORLD, AND PROCLAIM THIS GOOD NEWS TO ALL PEOPLE. THOSE THAT BELIEVE AND ARE BAPTIZED WILL DISCOVER SALVATION; BUT THOSE THAT BELIEVE NOT WILL BE LOST.

ATTEND THE PROMISE OF THE FATHER, WHICH YOU HAVE HEARD FROM ME. JOHN, CALLED THE BAPTISER, CLEANSED HIS FOLLOWERS BY IMMERSING THEM IN WATER, BUT YOU WILL BE MADE NEW BY THE VERY BREATH OF GOD.

YOU WILL RECEIVE NEW POWER WHEN THE BREATH OF GOD HAS COME AMONG YOU; AND YOU WILL BE MY WITNESSES, BEGINNING HERE IN JERUSALEM, JUDEA, AND SAMARIA, TO THE UTTERMOST PARTS OF THE EARTH.

BREATHE DEEP THE BREATH OF GOD. TEACH, EVEN AS I HAVE TAUGHT YOU. AND REMEMBER THAT I AM WITH YOU ALWAYS, EVEN TO THE END OF THE WORLD.

RECEIVE THE HOLY SPIRIT!

Index of references

PART 1:
WHO DO YOU SAY
THAT I AM?

THE PROBLEM OF RELIGION

1. Matthew 16:6
2. Matthew 16:9-11
3. Mark 7:7-9
4. Matthew 7:15; John 8:44
5. Matthew 23:13, 15, 14
6. Matthew 23:14
7. Matthew 23:16
8. Matthew 23:17
9. Matthew 23:18
10. Matthew 23:19
11. Matthew 23:20-22
12. Matthew 23:23
13. Matthew 23:24-26
14. Matthew 23:27-28
15. Matthew 23:29-30
16. Matthew 23:31-33
17. Matthew 23:34
18. Matthew 15:7-8 (Isaiah 29:13)
19. Luke 16:15
20. Matthew 8:11-12; 5:20

THE LIGHT THAT HAS
LIGHTED THE WORLD

1. John 12:46; 8:12; 9:5
2. John 5:33, 35-36
3. John10:37-38
4. Matthew 6:22-23
5. John 11:9-10; 12:35;
   Matthew 15:14; 5:15;
   Luke 8:16
6. John 12:36; Matthew 5:16
7. Luke 8:17; Matthew 10:27

THE REVELATION

1. John 12:23
2. John 8:50
3. John 8:17, 18; John 5:32, 34
4. John 7:18
5. John 7:28; 6:38; 18:37
6. John 10:30; 5:43; 10:10
7. John 28:18; 16:19;
   John 10:28; 14:27; Luke 10:19
8. John 8:32, 36; 5:35
9. John 6:40; 9:35-36

THE LIVING WORD

1. John 12:49-50
2. John 14:24; 5:24
3. John 5:25
4. John 5:39-40
5. John 5:37, 10:36
6. John 14:6, 6:63
7. John 12:47-48
8. Matthew 24:35

THE FATHER

1. Matthew 22:42
2. Matthew 11:27, John 7:29
3. John 8:29, 14:19-20
4. John 10:30; 16:28
5. John 5:19-21
6. John 5:26-27
7. John 8:26
8. John 8:28

THE GOOD SHEPHERD

1. Luke 12:32
2. John 10:14-16, 27-29
3. John 10:2-5
4. John 10:11-12
5. John 10:7, 1, 8-9
6. John 10:10

FOOD FOR THE SOUL

1. Matthew 4:4 (Deuteronomy 8:3)
2. John 6:35, 51, 48, 63, 50
3. John 6:27
4. John 6:49, 32-33
5. John 4:10, 13-14
6. John 7:37-38

PART 2:
THE NEW KINGDOM

THE KINGDOM OF HEAVEN

1. Matthew 11:12
2. Matthew 13:24-27
3. Matthew 13:28
4. Matthew 13:28
5. Matthew 13:29-30
6. Matthew 13:37-43
7. Matthew 12:25-26
8. Matthew 12:27
9. Matthew 12:28
10. Matthew 21:42-43
11. Mark 3:28-29; Matthew 21:31
12. Matthew 7:21
13. Luke 13:25
14. Luke 13:25
15. Luke 13:26
16. Luke 13:27
17. Matthew 7:22
18. Matthew 7:23
19. Luke 8:10; Matthew 13:35; (Psalm 78:1-3)
20. Matthew 25:14-15
21. Matthew 25:16-18
22. Matthew 25:19
23. Matthew 25:20-21
24. Matthew 25:22
25. Matthew 25:23
26. Matthew 25:24-25
27. Matthew 25:26-28
28. Matthew 25:29-30
29. Matthew 20:1-2
30. Matthew 20:3-4
31. Matthew 20:5-6
32. Matthew 20:7
33. Matthew 20:7
34. Matthew 20:8
35. Matthew 20:9-10

36. Matthew 20:11-12
37. Matthew 20:13-15
38. Matthew 20:16
39. Matthew 13:44
40. Matthew 13:45-46
41. Mark 4:26-29
42. Mark 4:31-32
43. Matthew 13:31-32
44. Matthew 13:33
45. Matthew 13:47-50
46. Luke 22:35
47. Matthew 6:34, 27
48. Matthew 6:26
49. Matthew 10:29, 31, 30
50. Matthew 6:28-30
51. Matthew 6:31-32
52. Matthew 6:33

THE ROYAL COMMANDMENT

1. Mark 12:29-30 (Deuteronomy 6:4)
2. Mark 12:31 (Leviticus 19:18)
3. Mark 12:31; John 15:12-13; Mark 12:31
4. Matthew 5:19; John 15:11
5. Matthew 5:43
6. Matthew 5:44-46
7. John 13:34-35; 14:23
8. John 14:23
9. John 16:27, 15:9-10
10. Luke 10:30-31
11. Luke 10:32
12. Luke 10:33-34
13. Luke 10:35
14. Luke 10:36
15. Luke 10:37

PART 3:
THE GREAT LESSONS

THE NEW DOCTRINE

1. Matthew 7:24
2. Matthew 7:25
3. Matthew 7:26-27
4. Luke 18:10-12
5. Luke 18:13
6. Luke 18:14
7. Luke 18:16-17
8. John 7:16-17
9. John 4:21-22
10. John 4:23-23, Luke 19:40
11. Matthew 12:3-5
12. Matthew 12:6-8
13. Matthew 12:11-12, John 7:24
14. John 7:16

THE BLESSINGS

1. Luke 11:28; Matthew 24:46
2. Matthew 5:3-8
3. Matthew 5:9-12; John 20:29;
   Matthew 13:16; 25:34

THE POWER OF PRAYER

1. John 16:24
2. Luke 11:5-6
3. Luke 11:7
4. Luke 11:8
5. Luke 11:9-10
6. Luke 18:2-4
7. Luke 18:4-5
8. Luke 18:7-8
9. Matthew 6:7-8
10. Matthew 21:13 (Isaiah 56:7)
11. Matthew 6:6; Mark 11:24;
    John 15:7
12. Matthew 6:9
13. Matthew 6:9
14. Matthew 6:10-13

THE TREASURES IN HEAVEN

1. Luke 6:31
2. Luke 16:19-21
3. Luke 16:22
4. Luke 16:23-24
5. Luke 16:25-26
6. Luke 16:27-28
7. Luke 16:29
8. Luke 16:30
9. Luke 16:31
10. Luke 6:34, 30
11. Mark 12:43-44
12. Mark 10:24, 25, 27
13. Matthew 6:19-21;
    Luke 12:33-34
14. Matthew 6:1-2
15. Matthew 6:3-4
16. Luke 6:38
17-19. Luke 12:16-21;
    Matthew 16:26

FAITH THAT MOVES
MOUNTAINS

1. Matthew 9:29
2. Matthew 8:11, 12
3. Matthew 18:19, 20
4. Mark 16:17-18
5. Matthew 17:20
6. Mark 11:24
7. Matthew 18:18
8. Mark 5:36; 9:23

PATIENCE, MERCY,
AND FORGIVENESS

1. John 20:23
2. Luke 7:41
3. Luke 7:41-42
4. Matthew 18:23-24
5. Matthew 18:25
6. Matthew 18:26
7. Matthew 18:27
8. Matthew 18:28
9. Matthew 18:29
10. Matthew 18:30
11. Matthew 18:31
12. Matthew 18:32-33
13. Matthew 18:34-35
14. Matthew 18:22; 5:25-26
15. Matthew 5:38-42

16. Mark 11:25;
   Matthew 5:23-24
17. Matthew 6:14

ON A FRUITFUL LIFE

1. Matthew 7:20
2. Matthew 5:13
3. Matthew 7:16-20
4. Luke 13:6-7
5. Luke 13:8-9
6. John 15:8; Matthew
   12:35
7. Matthew 13:3-7
8. Matthew 13:8
9. Matthew 13:19
10. Matthew 13:20-21
11. Matthew 13:22
12. Matthew 13:23

HEALTH AND HEALING
FOR BODY AND SOUL

1. Matthew 9:12
2. Matthew 9:13
3. Matthew 9:5
4. Matthew 9:6, 2; 8:13;
   Luke 8:48
5. Luke 15:4-6
6. Luke 15:7
7. Luke 15:8
8. Luke 15:9
9. Luke 15:10

PART 4:
THE CALL TO A NEW LIFE

THE CALL

1. John 15:16
2. Matthew 21:28
3. Matthew 21:29
4. Matthew 21:30
5. Matthew 21:30 – 31
6. Mark 10:18-19, 21
7. Matthew 16:24-25
8. Matthew 22:2-3
9. Matthew 22:4
10. Matthew 22:5-6
11. Matthew 22:7
12. Matthew 22:8-9
13. Matthew 22:10
14. Matthew 22:11-12
15. Matthew 22:13
16. John 15:19; Mark 1:15
17. John 6:44, 37
18. John 1:50
19. Matthew 7:13-14; Luke
   13:24

ON BEING BORN A SECOND
TIME

1. John 3:7
2. John 3:3, 5
3. John 3:6, 8
4. Matthew 9:16-17
5. John 3:10, 12
6. John 3:17-18
7. John 11:25-26, 40
8. John 6:29

9. Luke 15:11-12
10. Luke 15:13-14
11. Luke 15:15-19
12. Luke 15:20
13. Luke 15:21
14. Luke 15:22-24
15. Luke 15:2416. Luke
   15:25-26
17. Luke 15:27
18. Luke 15:28
19. Luke 15:29-30
20. Luke 15:31-32
21. Matthew 18:3, 11, 14
22. John 3:16

DISCIPLES AND SERVANTS

1. Matthew 6:24
2. Luke 14:28-30
3. Luke 14:31-32
4. Luke 14:33
5. Luke 16:10-12
6. Matthew 10:16
7. Mark 10:42-45
8. John 13:17; 8: 31
9. Matthew 23:3-8
10. Matthew 23:9-12
11. Matthew 25:31-33
12. Matthew 25:34-36
13. Matthew 25:37-39
14. Matthew 25:40
15. Matthew 25:41-43
16. Matthew 25:44
17. Matthew 25:45
18. Matthew 25:46
19. John 13:13-15

THE GREAT COMMISSION

1. Luke 9:60
2. Luke 10:2; 9:62
3. John 14:12; 12:26
4. Matthew 10:7
5. Matthew 10:8
6. Matthew 12:30
7. Luke 10:5-6
8. Luke 10:7
9. Luke 13:20
10. Matthew 10:17-18
11. Matthew 10:19-20;
   John 15:20-21
12. John 15:22, 24-25
   (Psalm 35:19)
13. Luke 12: 49, 51-52;
   John 15:18;
   Matthew 10:23, 14-15
14. Luke 10:16; Matthew
   10:22
15. John 16:33

CHRIST'S PRAYER FOR HIS
DISCIPLES

1. John 17:1-2
2. John 17:3-8
3. John 17:9-11
4. John 17:12-13
5. John 17:14-17
6. John 17:18-21
7. John 17:22-24
8. John 17:25-26

PART 5:
THE PROMISE

THIS GENERATION

1. Mark 8:38
2. Matthew 12:39-40
3. Matthew 12:41
4. Matthew 12:42
5. Matthew 11:16-17
6. Matthew 11:18
7. Matthew 11:19
8. Matthew 12:34
9. Matthew 16:2-3
10. Matthew 16:3
11. Matthew 11:28-30
12. Matthew 19:28

A PLACE FOR YOU

1. John 14:2
2. John 14:3, 1, 2, 28
3. John 16:19-20
4. John 16:21-22

THE PROMISE OF THE SPIRIT

1. John 6:63
2. John 14:15-17
3. John 14:18; 16: 7
4. John 16:8-11
5. John 16:12-13
6. John 16:14-15; Luke
   11:11-12
7. Luke 11:13
8. John 15:26; 14:26

AN INVITATION TO LIFE

1. John 3:16
2. Luke 14:16-17
3. Luke 14:18
4. Luke 14:18
5. Luke 14:19
6. Luke 14:20
7. Luke 14:21
8. Luke 14:22
9. Luke 14:23-24
10. John 5:24, 28, 25, 29
11. John 17:3; 3:16;
   Matthew 24:14

THE END TIMES

1. Matthew 24:34
2. Matthew 21:33
3. Matthew 21:34-35
4. Matthew 21:36
5. Matthew 21:37
6. Matthew 21:38
7. Matthew 21:39-40
8. Luke 13:34-35
9. Luke 19:42; 21:26
10. Matthew 24:15-22
11. Luke 19:43-44
12. Matthew 24:2; Luke
   21:24
13. Luke 21:9-11, 25;
   Matthew 24:7-8, 12
14. Matthew 24:9; Luke
   21:36
15. Matthew 24:32, 36, 34

THE RETURN

1. Matthew 24:42

2. Matthew 24:4-5, 11
3. Matthew 24:23-24
4. Matthew 24:26-27
5. Matthew 24:30; 26:64;
   24:31; 16:27
6. Matthew 24:37-38
7. Luke 17:28-30
8. Luke 21:34-35
9. Matthew 24:40-43
10. Luke 10:24; Matthew
   24:44
11. Matthew 25:1-5
12. Matthew 25:6
13. Matthew 25:7-8
14. Matthew 25:9
15. Matthew 25:10
16. Matthew 25:11
17. Matthew 25:12
18. Luke 12:37
19. Matthew 25:13; Luke
   12:35-36
20. Luke 16:17

PART 6:
THE LAST DAYS OF CHRIST
ON THE EARTH

THE BETRAYAL

1. Luke 18:31-33
2. John 13:33; Luke 22:15-
   16, 18
3. Luke 22:19-20
4. Matthew 26:24; John
   13:18-19
5. John 13:38; Mark 14:27
   (Zachariah 13:7)
6. Mark 14:36
7. Mark 14:41; Matthew
   26:52
8. Luke 22:48, 52-53
9. Matthew 26:53-54; John
   13:31

THE TRIAL AND THE CROSS

1. John 19:11
2. John 18:21, 20
3. John 18:23
4. John 18:36-37; 12:31-32
5. John 10:17-18
6. Luke 23:34
7. Matthew 27:46

FOLLOWING THE
RESURRECTION

1. Luke 24:25-26; John
   20:27
2. Luke 24:44, 46-47
3. John 8:14, 23
4. John 3:13, 20:17
5. Luke 24:38, 36, 39; John
   20:29
6. John 14:19

ALWAYS

1. John 20:21
2. Matthew 28:19;
   Mark 16:15 – 16
3. Acts 1:4-5
4. Acts 1:8
5. Matthew 28:20
6. John 20:22

ABOUT THE AUTHOR

Lee Cantelon was born in the United States, but was raised in Germany, Belgium, and Switzerland. He attended the UCLA film school in Los Angeles before returning to Europe, where he produced and directed a number of weekly television programs for both French and Italian television, featuring discussions about religion, the arts, philosophy, and culture from a religious perspective.

In the late 1980s, he began work on *The Words* following a conversation with a friend in London, who was engaged in a long and hapless quest for spiritual fulfillment. Lee's response, the draft manuscript for *The Words*, became a reply to the many people he had met who were put off by the organized church and religion, but remained curious concerning the core message of Christianity, and more precisely, what Jesus had said. In *The Words*, he compiled Jesus' words thematically, in clear and modern English, for non-Christians, spiritual seekers, agnostics, and believers.

Since its first publishing in the 1990s, *The Words* has been translated into more than twenty languages, including Arabic and Chinese. Much to the author's surprise, it was awarded the Nihil Obstat and Imprimatur by the Catholic Church, and in recent years, has inspired two music projects, *The Sermon on Exposition Boulevard*, with his friend Rickie Lee Jones, and *Wordz from the Street*, a rap album that features many of the most prominent contemporary rap artists, reciting and improvising from the pages of this book.

Lee lives in Hollywood, California, where he publishes two Web sites based on *The Words* (www. thewords.com and www.thewordstoday.com). He shares his apartment with his dog, Quincy, and a nearly constant influx of guests and friends. His passions are photography (his photographs can be viewed on *The Words* Web site at www.thewords.com) and fixed-gear bicycles.

ABOUT THE DESIGNER

Since 1981 Mark Arnold has worked at internationally respected advertising agencies TBWA / Chiat Day and CORE, among others, where his print and television work on a wide variety of accounts such as the NFL, The Ford Motor Company, Indian Motorcycles, and Winchester Ammunition has won many national and international awards.

Mark left CORE in 2001 to pursue work with non-profits and biblically based organizations. Mark created a visual edition of Philip Yancey's gold medallion book *What's So Amazing About Grace?* (www.visualgracebook.com) that is "visually, intellectually, and emotionally stimulating so you can't put it down." In 2006, Mark completed a visual edition of Lee Strobel's best-selling book *The Case for Faith* (www.visualfaithbook.com).

Mark is pleased to be a part of *The Words* project and hopes that his choice of typefaces and the rawness of the design evoke the counterculture power of Jesus' message.

Mark currently lives in Webster Groves, a historic community in St. Louis, Missouri, with his wife of 25 years and their three energetic teenage sons. Samples of his work can be seen at www.andarnold.com.

ABOUT THE BOOK

In the 1990s, I organized the words of Jesus, as recorded in the Gospels, into a concise book, with the intention to make available the message of Christ to non-religious readers, persons curious about the meaning and depth of Christ's words, who found themselves alienated from organized church and religion. The result has generated a great deal of interest outside the Christian tradition, and exposed the words of Jesus to many non-traditional readers.

During the process, I partnered with many Bible translators and commentary writers, from a very wide range of scholarship that reached from the Hebrew University in Jerusalem, to Fuller Seminary, in Pasadena, California (with many links in between). The final product, The Words, offers the message of Christ in expressive language that is easy to understand.

While the entire gospel narrative is a part of Christian theology, it is Jesus' words in and of themselves that teach believers how to live and how faith makes a difference in their lives. Jesus' message is full of surprises and is often challenging. At times, his words confront the modern church and their practices "in his name." Compared to the tradition that has grown up around his teachings, they strike me as remarkably simple, straightforward, and filled with wisdom.

I would like to thank my father, Willard Cantelon, and my mother, Verna, for encouraging me to answer one friend's sincere question. I cannot adequately thank all of the translators and wonderful hearts and minds that assisted with the completion of this book, but will mention a few. Thanks to my dear friend, MacArthur Jollay, for introducing me to William Barclay, to Ray Pritz for inviting me to Jerusalem, and for taking the manuscript to his colleagues at the Hebrew University, and to Rabbi Joshua O. Haberman, and Amy Leavitt.

Special thanks to Craig and Sandy Hoekenga for believing that this was a book that needed to happen, to Rev. D. W. Cover and his staff, and to Norman Correll. Thanks to David Sanford and Tim Beals for making this book possible. In closing, thank you David and Dee Dee Murry for carrying on the vision that Barry held close to his heart, and Rickie, for putting music to these ancient and stirring words.

– Lee Cantelon

AFTERWORD

AS ARGUABLY THE MOST CONTROVERSIAL AND MISUNDERSTOOD FIGURE IN THE HISTORY OF CIVILIZATION, Jesus of Nazareth and the words he spoke have been twisted, stretched, perverted and, at times, all but drowned out in official proclamations and seemingly contradictory explanations by those who claim to know for certain what they mean.

Yet *The Words* presents them in a much quieter manner, simply for what they are in themselves—no propaganda. There is nothing attached to the words but the voice of the man who uttered them some two thousand years ago. *The Words* offers us a view of a teacher who saw God as his own father, one who offered love, hope, and acceptance. Jesus' words, in this beautifully and hiply designed volume are, in effect, wonderfully simple, and simply confounding in their directness, and in suggesting a way through the confusion and suspicion by their very quietness and unadorned speech.

The words are here to accept, ignore or reject at will. If they are to be considered, it is not because of the dazzle of their verbal presentation; but simply as an introduction, a conversation starter. Here is a place to rest while encountering something very old and covered over, stripped of its usual trappings and presented simply for your perusal, consideration, and perhaps even delight.

—THOM JUREK, *Senior Writer*
All-Music Guide (www.allmusic.com)